Inviting People to Christ

Books in the Stephen Olford Biblical Preaching Library

Believing Our Beliefs
Biblical Answers to Personal Problems
Committed to Christ and His Church
Fresh Lessons from Former Leaders
Living Words and Loving Deeds
Proclaiming the Good News
The Pulpit and the Christian Calendar 1
The Pulpit and the Christian Calendar 2
The Pulpit and the Christian Calendar 3

Inviting People to Christ

Evangelistic Expository Messages

Stephen F. Olford

 Baker Books

A Division of Baker Book House Co
Grand Rapids, Michigan 49516

© 1998 by Stephen F. Olford

Published by Baker Books
a division of Baker Book House Company
P.O. Box 6287, Grand Rapids, MI 49516-6287

Printed in the United States of America

ISBN 0-8010-9062-8

Scripture quotations are taken from the New King James Version. Copyright © 1979, 1980, 1982 by Thomas Nelson, Inc., Publishers. Used by permission. All rights reserved.

For current information about all releases from Baker Book House, visit our web site:

http://www.bakerbooks.com

Contents

Grateful Acknowledgments   7

Introduction   9

1. The Grace of God (Titus 2:11–15; John 1:14–18)   11
2. Forgiveness Full and Free (Acts 10:34–43)   20
3. The Savior of Sinners (1 Timothy 1:12–17)   28
4. We Must Glory in the Cross (Galatians 6:11–18)   36
5. The Fate of Fruitlessness (Mark 11:12–14, 20–26)   46
6. What the Bible Says about Saving Faith (Romans 10:1–21)   56
7. The Person Whom God Accepts (Luke 18:9–14)   64
8. Spiritual Security (John 10:14–18, 26–30)   72
9. Is There a Heaven to Gain? (John 14:1–6)   80
10. Is There a Hell to Shun? (Luke 16:19–31)   90
11. The Confession of Sin (Proverbs 28:11–14)   100
12. God's New Creation (2 Corinthians 5:16–21)   109
13. Life with a Minus (Mark 10:17–25)   116

Notes   125

95705

Grateful Acknowledgments

The expository outlines of evangelistic sermons in this book are the finished product of messages delivered extemporaneously to Crusade audiences around the world and in the churches I have served. In the "flow" of such preaching, many quotes, concepts, and illustrations were brought to mind without specific documentation. I, therefore, acknowledge gratefully all sources of such material—heard or read—from the "gifts to men" (Eph. 4:8) with which our risen Lord has enriched the church.

Stephen F. Olford

Introduction

Preach the word. . . . *Do* the work of an evangelist" (2 Tim. 4:2, 5, italics mine). These two imperatives are as relevant today as when the great apostle Paul first dictated them. Even if a pastor/preacher does not consider himself an evangelist in the sense in which Philip was gifted (Acts 21:8), he is still mandated to "do the work of an evangelist." To reach the people and preach the gospel, is our duty to God and our debt to humanity—in the local church and in the global ministry.

The evangelistic expositions offered in this second volume of two (volume 1 is titled *Proclaiming the Good News*) are messages I actually preached at our evening "Witness" service at Calvary Baptist Church in New York City, and God was graciously pleased to bless them to the salvation of souls. Now it's your turn!

The Subjects. These are varied but *vital* in substance and scope. In adopting and adapting these subjects for your own preaching ministry, you may want to change titles and, therefore, modify structure. By all means do this—as long as you *are true to the text!*

The Sermons. Even though the thirteen sermons are individual messages, each one is an *exposition*. Whether in the churches I served in the U.K., at Calvary Baptist Church in New York, or during crusades around the world, I have *never* preached an evangelistic sermon that was *not expository*. God has not promised to bless what *we* say but He has promised to bless what He has forever said in His Son and in His Word.

The sermons do not constitute a series per se nor are they individual *topical* sermons. Each message is an expository treatment of a gospel theme—with its own call to decision. For this reason, there is no designed sequence that you need to follow.

The Spirit. Paul reminds us that "the letter kills, but the Spirit gives life" (2 Cor. 3:6). Words, *in and of themselves,* cannot produce the fruits of righteousness in the lives of those to whom we minister, even though they may be divine oracles. There has to be the vitalizing Spirit to charge the words with life-transforming power. The apostle states this clearly when writing to the Thessalonians. Mark his language: "Our gospel did not come to you *in word only,* but also in power, and in the Holy Spirit" (1 Thess. 1:5, italics mine). So as you expound these evangelistic sermons, make sure that you claim "the Promise of [the] Father"—even the endowment "with power from on high" (Luke 24:49).

Blessings on you as you preach!

1

The Grace of God

Titus 2:11–15; John 1:14–18

For the grace of God that brings salvation has appeared to all men, teaching us that, denying ungodliness and worldly lusts, we should live soberly, righteously, and godly in the present age.

Titus 2:11–12

Introduction

There is no New Testament writer who excels in expounding this matchless subject of the grace of God like the apostle Paul. He who himself was a recipient of that grace could say, "But by the grace of God I am what I am" (1 Cor. 15:10). He writes of the grace that justifies, for we are "justified freely by His grace" (Rom. 3:24). He elevates the grace of God to show it against the heinousness of sin, for "where sin abounded, grace abounded much more" (Rom. 5:20). And he brings us face to face with the Savior Himself, saying, "For you know the grace of our Lord Jesus Christ, that though He was rich, yet for your sakes He became poor, that you through His poverty might become rich" (2 Cor. 8:9). Again he tells us that "by grace you have been saved through faith, and that not of yourselves; it is the gift of God, not of works, lest anyone should boast" (Eph. 2:8–9).

I want to speak now of the grace of God in action, the river of active love, flowing from the throne of God to the heart of the needy sinner. Grace is glory in the bud; and glory is grace in full bloom. This outworking of grace operates in a threefold way. Observe in the first place:

I. Grace Liberates Men and Women

"For the grace of God that brings salvation has appeared to all men, . . . [in the person of] our great God and Savior Jesus Christ, who gave Himself for us, that He might *redeem* us from every lawless deed" (Titus 2:11, 13–14, italics mine). Our "great God and Savior Jesus Christ" through grace redeems us and acquits us:

A. Redeems Us from the Slavery of Sin

"Whoever commits sin is a slave of sin" (John 8:34). The purpose for which the Savior died on Calvary was that He might pay the ransom price, to buy us out of slavery. "I am . . . sold under sin," says Paul in Romans 7:14. And this is true of every man, woman, or child, however cultured or refined, who is out of Christ. They are in the slave market of sin.

Perhaps you have not realized that this explains your slavery to pride, jealousy, quick temper, and other vices and habits that have spoiled your life. But the Lord Jesus Christ has come to redeem you from the slavery of sin. "You were not redeemed with corruptible things, like silver or gold, . . . but with the precious blood of Christ, as of a lamb without blemish and without spot" (1 Peter 1:18–19).

Illustration

John Newton was the son of a sea captain engaged in the slave trade. After his mother died when he was six, he completed two years of school and joined his father's ship at the age of eleven. Immorality, debauchery, and failure followed. Rejected by his father and finally jailed and degraded, Newton later served on slave ships where he so incurred the hatred of his employer's Negro wife that he became a "slave of slaves."

His conversion was the result of a violent storm in which he almost lost his life. At the age of thirty-nine he became a minister of the gospel and was a pastor for fifteen years. He wrote many hymns. His personal experience is recounted in the world-famous hymn:

> Amazing grace! how sweet the sound,
> That saved a wretch like me!
> I once was lost, but now am found,
> Was blind, but now I see.
>
> 'Twas grace that taught my heart to fear,
> And grace my fears relieved;
> How precious did that grace appear
> The hour I first believed!
>
> The Lord has promised good to me,
> His word my hope secures;
> He will my shield and portion be
> As long as life endures.
>
> Through many dangers, toils and snares,
> I have already come;
> 'Tis grace hath brought me safe thus far,
> And grace will lead me home.
>
> When we've been there ten thousand years,
> Bright shining as the sun,

> We've no less days to sing God's praise
> Than when we'd first begun.

Divine grace through Christ also:

B. Acquits Us of the Sentence of Sin

"If the Son makes you free, you shall be free indeed" (John 8:36). The Lord Jesus has not only bought us out of slavery by paying the price of redemption, but set us free from the sentence of death that works in us. As a living, triumphant Savior, He is "just and the justifier" of those who believe in Him (Rom. 3:26). As the Son in His own house, He acquits us by saying, "Slave, you are free!" How wonderful is the grace of God in Jesus Christ!

Illustration

Tell the story of the scapegoat (Lev. 16:8–22) and illustrate the remitting of sin by the release of the goat into the wilderness (see verse 22).

Grace more than liberates; it also educates.

II. Grace Educates Men and Women

"The grace of God . . . has appeared . . . teaching [or educating] us" (Titus 2:11–12). The Lord Jesus has given Himself for us, to "purify for Himself" (v. 14) a people for His possession. The meaning of that phrase suggests cleansing by the Word or sanctifying through the truth.

A. Grace Educates Us to Deny What God Condemns

Amplification

Define and develop *godlessness* or *ungodliness* as: 1. general impiety (Rom. 1:18; 11:26; 2 Tim. 2:16; Titus 2:12; 2. ungodly deeds (Jude 15)—"works of ungodliness"

in the Revised Version; 3. lusts and desires after evil things
(Jude 18).

1. GODLESSNESS

"Denying ungodliness and worldly lusts" (Titus 2:12).
Sin has ruined not only our character but also our conduct, so that we are unlike God. But the disciplining
grace of God enables us to overcome that which mars
our life.

2. WORLDLINESS

By *worldliness* is meant, no doubt, that which the
apostle John speaks of when he says, "For all that is
in the world—the lust of the flesh, the lust of the eyes,
and the pride of life—is not of the Father but is of the
world" (1 John 2:16). There are the:

• Worldly Perversions

"The lust of the flesh"; these are appetites and desires
that are perverse and misdirected—unholy tastes for
things that are harmful.

• Worldly Distractions

"The lust of the eyes"; these are the things of the
world that attract, seduce, and allure the would-be
Christian. But alas, they are transient and empty; and
behind them is the loud laugh of the devil.

• Worldly Ambitions

"The pride of life"; this is the assertive ego that
grasps at glory and longs for prominence. But by the
grace of God worldly perversions, distractions, and
ambitions can be conquered. So with the apostle Paul
we can say, "I also count all things loss for the excel-
lence of the knowledge of Christ Jesus my Lord . . .
that I may know Him and the power of His resurrection, and the fellowship of His sufferings, being conformed to His death" (Phil. 3:8, 10).

So the educating grace of God teaches us that which we are to deny and:

B. Grace Educates Us to Develop What God Commends

1. A SOBERNESS OF LIFE IN RELATION TO OURSELVES

"Teaching [or educating] us that . . . we should live soberly, righteously, and godly in the present age" (Titus 2:12). This is the self-control that comes only by the grace of God operating in us. A man came to me some time ago and said, "If you could introduce me to an experience that would bring self-mastery to my life, I would give my right hand for it."

Illustration

Seven months before his death from AIDS a young man wrote of the freedom from sin that Jesus can give: "Up until seven years ago I was actively homosexual. I was saved, but not walking with Christ. When I came to my spiritual senses and turned my back on it—oh, the joy of being forgiven! The release of that terrible burden of hideous sin! Even today, all these years later, in prayer I frequently weep and literally sob with joy at the mercy of God. This disease and the knowledge of my shortened life are absolutely nothing compared with the knowledge that I will be going to meet my Savior and my Father pure and unblemished."[1]

2. A RIGHTEOUSNESS OF LIFE IN RELATION TO OTHERS

"We should live . . . righteously." O the clashes, schisms, and divisions in human life everywhere! Husbands and wives cannot live together; employers and employees cannot get on together. But the grace of God has appeared, breaking into the darkness of man's unrest and turmoil and teaching us to live righteously.

3. A HOLINESS OF LIFE IN RELATION TO GOD

"We should live . . . godly." This is taking on our-selves the character and likeness of Jesus Christ. The more we look into His face and catch the glory of His presence, and the more we understand His Word, the more His likeness is stamped on us.

So the grace of God liberates, educates, and brings us into those "good works, which God prepared before-hand that we should walk in them" (Eph. 2:10).

Grace liberates, educates, and then:

III. Grace Consecrates Men and Women

"Who gave Himself for us, that He might redeem us from every lawless deed and purify for Himself His own special people, zealous for good works" (Titus 2:14). We sometimes sing:

> I am Thine, O Lord, I have heard Thy voice,
> And it told Thy love to me;
> But I long to rise in the arms of faith,
> And be closer drawn to Thee.
>
> Consecrate me now to Thy service, Lord,
> By the power of grace divine;
> Let my soul look up with a steadfast hope,
> And my will be lost in Thine.
>
> Fanny Crosby

Service by the grace of God should be characterized by:

A. Fervency of Spirit

"*Zealous* for good works." For Paul there was a spe-cial significance in that word *zealous*. There was a time when he was fired with a wrong zeal, causing havoc in the church of Jesus Christ. But now he wanted his zeal to be harnessed and consecrated to the One whom he had wronged.

For every man and woman, boy and girl in the purpose of God's electing grace, there is a glorious ministry already prepared. Long before you were born, God had a plan for your life, good works that you should fulfill. And he wants from you a service that is born of reciprocal love. Your language should be:

> Were the whole realm of nature mine,
> That were a present far too small;
> Love so amazing, so divine,
> Demands my soul, my life, my all.
>
> Isaac Watts

Out of love for such unbounded grace, we should serve with fervency of spirit. This was, of course, characteristic of our blessed Master. There were times when He could not even eat because of the pressure of the demands on Him. There were times when, because of His zeal, His family said He had a devil. And at other times, even His disciples could not understand it, till they remembered that it was written of Him, "Zeal for Your house has eaten Me up [or consumed me]" (John 2:17). Paul says that we should be "not lagging in diligence, fervent in spirit, serving the Lord" (Rom. 12:11). It is the picture of the boiling kettle—no cooling off, no lukewarmness, no halfheartedness. For Paul knew, as did John when he was given the revelation of the risen Christ, that the Savior cannot stand lukewarmness. He would have us either stone cold or fervently hot.

With fervency of spirit, there should be:

B. Faithfulness in Service

"Zealous for *good works*." Every true servant longs to hear, "Well done, good and faithful servant. . . . Enter into the joy of your lord" (Matt. 25:21). The person who knows something of the grace of God will be faithful in service, whether it is at noonday or midnight, on the mountaintop or in the valley. It is faithfulness that counts, rather than success.

Illustration

A young Christian soldier in the army was often assaulted by his tent-mates while at prayer at night. He sought advice of his chaplain, and by his counsel omitted his usual habit. His ardent heart could not endure this. He chose rather to have prayer with persecution than peace without, and he resumed his old way. The result was that, after a time, all his ten or twelve companions knelt in prayer with him. In reporting to his chaplain he said, "Isn't it better to keep the colors flying?"[2]

Now it is characteristic of the apostle Paul that, in speaking of the grace of God, he should personify it. He says, "the grace of God . . . has appeared" (Titus 2:11), as if it were a person who has appeared; and indeed it is. For he goes on to speak of "our great God and Savior Jesus Christ" (v. 13). That brings us to those wonderful words in John's Gospel, "And the Word became flesh and dwelt among us, . . . full of grace and truth" (John 1:14). And again, "And of His fullness we have all received, and grace for grace" (v. 16). My friend, have you received the grace of God in Jesus Christ? "He came to His own, and His own did not receive Him. But as many as received Him, to them He gave the right to become children of God, to those who believe in His name" (vv. 11–12).

Conclusion

Jesus stands among us in his risen power. Receive Him now and close in with the overtures of grace.

Forgiveness Full and Free

Acts 10:34–43

To Him all the prophets witness that, through His name, whoever believes in Him will receive remission of sins.

Acts 10:43

Introduction

The context in which our passage is found is both interesting and important. Peter the apostle had been divinely commissioned to go to the house of a man in Caesarea named Cornelius, a centurion of a cohort called the Italian Regiment. He was a devout man; he and his household feared God. What is more, he was known for his generous giving to people in need. But even with his good works he did not know peace with God; with all his religion he had not yet experienced the calm of sins forgiven. So Peter came to his home and preached the gospel to him. The text before us forms the climax of the message of good news that Cornelius heard that day. Let us consider it in detail.

"To Him all the prophets witness that, through His name, whoever believes in Him will receive remission of sins." Consider, first of all:

I. The Promise of Forgiveness

"To Him all the prophets witness" (Acts 10:43). Here Peter is referring to the Old Testament Scriptures, which promise forgiveness through the coming Messiah. These Scriptures were divided into three parts: the book of the Law, the book of the Psalms, and the book of the Prophets. A study of these sections of the Bible makes it evident that forgiveness was ever and always the promise of God for men and women.

A. Forgiveness Was Promised in the Book of the Law

Listen to these words: "The LORD is longsuffering and abundant in mercy, forgiving iniquity and transgression; but He by no means clears the guilty" (Num. 14:18). Could any statement be clearer on the matter of forgiveness? In these words of Moses we learn that God can never overlook sin; He must judge it. But despite the demands of His holiness, He is longsuffering and of great mercy, forgiving iniquity and transgression.

This explains why the entire system of sacrifice and offering was practiced throughout Old Testament times. Sin had to be atoned for, and the animal victims were but a foreshadowing of the one and only sacrifice that was to be offered in the person of our Lord and Savior Jesus Christ.

B. Forgiveness Was Promised in the Book of the Psalms

Mark these words: "If you, LORD, should mark iniquities, O Lord, who could stand? But there is forgiveness with You, that You may be feared" (Ps. 130:3–4). The poets and singers of Israel expressed the same truth that with God there is forgiveness through a promised and provided sacrifice. David could exclaim, "Blessed [happy] is he whose transgression is forgiven" (Ps. 32:1).

C. Forgiveness Was Promised in the Book of the Prophets

Hear the words of Isaiah when he declared, "Let the wicked forsake his way, and the unrighteous man his thoughts; let him return to the LORD, and He will have mercy on him; and to our God, for He will abundantly pardon" (Isa. 55:7). The same prophet assures us that such pardon and forgiveness are possible only because God had provided a Bearer away of sins. So we hear him saying, "But He was wounded for our transgressions, He was bruised for our iniquities; the chastisement for our peace was upon Him, and by His stripes we are healed" (Isa. 53:5).

Here, then, is the significance of Peter's statement, "To Him all the prophets witness that, through His name, whoever believes in Him will receive remission of sins" (Acts 10:43). Throughout Old Testament Scriptures the message was ever clear and plain that God was sending His own Son to become the Savior of the world.

But now look at the second part of the verse:

II. The Provision of Forgiveness

"To Him all the prophets witness that, *through His name,* whoever believes in Him will receive remission of sins" (Acts 10:43, italics mine). When the fullness of time was come, the promised Messiah arrived, and through Him God effected the necessary work that made forgiveness possible for men and women, boys and girls. The phrase "through

His name" comprehends the total life and ministry of the Lord Jesus Christ. So we find that:

A. Through the Coming of Christ Forgiveness Was Made Possible

The angel's message at the birth of Christ was unmistakably clear: "You shall call His name JESUS, for He will save His people from their sins" (Matt. 1:21). Up until that time God's ancient people depended on animal sacrifices, but we are told, "It is not possible that the blood of bulls and goats could take away sins. . . . But this Man, after He had offered one sacrifice for sins forever, sat down at the right hand of God" (Heb. 10:4, 12). The blood of bulls and goats temporarily covered sins but could not take them away. At last, however, there appeared the Messiah Himself. Pointing Him out, John the Baptist could declare, "Behold! The Lamb of God who takes away the sin of the world!" (John 1:29). So His coming made forgiveness possible.

B. Through the Living of Christ Forgiveness Was Made Personal

Looking into the face of a paralyzed man whose sense of guilt was worse than his physical disability, Jesus said, "Man, your sins are forgiven you" (Luke 5:20). And when the Master was questioned as to His authority for such an astonishing statement, He pointed to Himself and said, "The Son of Man has power on earth to forgive sins" (v. 24).

So men and women were made aware of the personal application of His forgiving word. Indeed, even the callous soldiers who were nailing Him to the cross heard Him cry, "Father, forgive them, for they do not know what they do" (Luke 23:34).

C. Through the Dying of Christ Forgiveness Was Made Purposeful

The Bible tells us that "without shedding of blood there is no remission" (Heb. 9:22). As we have seen already,

God is "of purer eyes than to behold evil, and cannot look on wickedness" (Hab. 1:13). Therefore sin had to be judged fully and finally in the person of a fit substitute, and there was only One who answered the qualification; it was the Lord Jesus Christ Himself. As the hymn writer expresses it:

> He died that we might be forgiven,
> He died to make us good,
> That we might go at last to heaven,
> Saved by His precious blood.
>
> There was no other good enough
> To pay the price of sin;
> He only could unlock the gate
> Of heaven and let us in.

Cecil F. Alexander

D. Through the Rising of Christ Forgiveness Was Made Practical

We read that God exalted Christ "to His right hand to be Prince and Savior, to give repentance to Israel and forgiveness of sins" (Acts 5:31). Because Jesus lives, forgiveness can be a practical experience to all who believe in Him. The resurrection of Jesus Christ is the evidence and seal of God's acceptance of the sacrifice He made for sin. Now in mercy, God can come out to meet the repentant sinner and grant him forgiveness and peace.

Illustration

Ted Timling spent twenty years as master of ceremonies of the prestigious Wimbledon Tennis Championships. Then in 1949 he committed an unpardonable breach of etiquette by outfitting the tennis player Sussie Moran in lace-trimmed "panties." Fired for his mistake, he lingered as an outcast for the next thirty-three years. Only in 1982 was he forgiven and reinstated. Wimbledon officials felt they had to protect the sanctity of their name. They also felt that a thirty-three-year exile from the club was a good dose of punishment.

God has no such fears! He is anxious that we receive His Son's instant, true, and refreshing forgiveness. His grace is greater than all our shame.

So we have seen something of the promise and provision of forgiveness. But now examine the closing part of our text:

III. The Possession of Forgiveness

"To Him all the prophets witness that, through His name, *whoever believes in Him will receive* remission of sins" (Acts 10:43, italics mine). How wonderful to know that what has been promised and provided can be possessed on the simple terms God has set forth in this verse! This act of believing involves two important conditions.

A. Radical Repentance of Sin

"Whoever believes in Him"; believing is always linked with repentance in the Bible. On the day of Pentecost Peter could say to his congregation, "Repent, and let every one of you be baptized in the name of Jesus Christ for the remission of sins; and you shall receive the gift of the Holy Spirit" (Acts 2:38).

Before a person can openly confess his faith in the Lord Jesus Christ he has to repent of his sins. This means more than being sorry or regretful over the past. It calls for a total change of heart, mind, and will concerning the question of sin. The Bible says, "He who covers his sins will not prosper, But whoever confesses and forsakes them will have mercy" (Prov. 28:13). John states the same thing when he writes, "If we confess our sins, He is faithful and just to forgive us our sins and to cleanse us from all unrighteousness" (1 John 1:9).

Perhaps the reason why you have never known the forgiveness of God is because you have never demonstrated your willingness and determination to turn your back on your sins.

Then there is a second condition:

B. Personal Reliance on Christ

"Whoever believes in Him will receive remission of sins." There is only one Person in the universe who can set you free from sin, and He is the Lord Jesus Christ. The apostle Paul makes this clear when he affirms, "In Him we have redemption through His blood, the forgiveness of sins, according to the riches of His grace" (Eph. 1:7).

Illustration

Carl Gustav Jung, psychiatrist and founder of the school of analytical psychology, had to come ultimately to this same conclusion concerning forgiveness. In the course of his work he discovered that while he was able to psychoanalyze problems, he could not remedy the sense of guilt. So after he had worked on his patients, he would recommend that his patients go and listen to the preaching of a certain minister who was strong on the message of forgiveness!

Conclusion

Here it is then—forgiveness full and free. Do you want to know forgiveness in your life? Well, the text says, "To Him all the prophets witness that, *through His name,* whoever believes in Him *will* receive remission of sins." We have looked at the promise; we have studied the provision, but what matters most is to possess forgiveness. Remember the conditions: a total repentance of sin and then a total reliance on Christ.

Illustration

In Old Testament times, a yearlong celebration called Jubilee was held every fifty years in which all slaves were freed, mortgaged lands were restored to their original owners, and the earth was left fallow (see Leviticus 25:8–17). It was a time of forgiveness, freedom, and rejoicing.

You can know your Jubilee today. Make your prayer:

> Forgiveness, full and free,
> God offers now to me;
> Because of Calvary—
> For me, it's Jubilee!

S. F. O.

The Savior of Sinners

1 Timothy 1:12–17

This is a faithful saying and worthy of all acceptance, that Christ Jesus came into the world to save sinners, of whom I am chief.

1 Timothy 1:15

Introduction

The text before us has been one of the great watchwords of the faith down through the centuries. Like the other "faithful sayings" found in the Pastoral Epistles, it constitutes a formula, expressing weighty and memorable truths, well known and often repeated by the brotherhood of Christians in the early church.

This particular saying was evidently and especially precious to the apostle Paul. The words "of whom I am chief" were not used rhetorically or extravagantly. He meant them from the heart. With all his religion, his boasted self-righteousness, and his acknowledged academic qualification, this man eventually came to see that he was a helpless and hopeless sinner, or—in his own language—the chief of sinners. We can, therefore, well understand the apostle glorying in a "faithful saying" that sets forth the Lord Jesus as the Savior of sinners. Please consider the Savior whom Paul exalts in this text. Observe, first of all:

I. The Revelation of the Savior

"Christ Jesus came" (1 Tim. 1:15). In these words we have the revelation of the Savior's:

A. Nativity

"Christ Jesus *came*." Yes, we know that He was born, but He *came* to be born! Herein is the mystery of the incarnation. No wonder Paul exclaimed, "And without controversy great is the mystery of godliness: God was manifested in the flesh" (1 Tim. 3:16).

Of all birthdays, the birthday of the Lord Jesus Christ is held in man's memory with highest regard. It is an extraordinary fact that in Western civilization, time is dated from the birth of Christ.

Some say that Christ was only a Jew, who, if He ever existed, was a peasant in an obscure province in a far-off age; who wrote no book, made no discovery, invented no philosophy, and built no temple; who, at the end, was forsaken by all His little band of followers and then died a criminal's death. Yet the centuries carry His signature; every year is called "the year of our Lord."

No one knows why or how or when or who did it. Emperors have endeavored to alter this reckoning, by dating time from their birth or coronation. Moslems have tried dating time from the flight of Mohammed from Mecca to Medina in A.D. 622. France, in 1793, decreed that time should date from the Revolution. And scientists have declared that time ought to be adjusted to the march of heavenly bodies. Yet today people throughout much of the world date time from the birth of our Lord

Jesus Christ. Indeed, even the infidel magazines that blaspheme His name are obliged to adjust their calendar to His cradle. Truly our Lord has put His signature on time itself. And until time shall be no more, every new year will be baptized into His name.

These words also give us a revelation of the Savior's:

B. Name

"Christ Jesus"—*Christ,* the Anointed One; *Jesus,* the Savior; *Christ Jesus,* the Anointed Savior—in this name we see His authority to *save.* And indeed, His is the only name that spells the answer to humanity's greatest need. Philosophers, physicians, psychologists, scientists, and religionists of all ages have tried to solve the problem of man's sin. They have failed, and their names mean nothing to us in this respect. But mention the name "Christ Jesus," and, with Paul, ten thousand times ten thousand voices cry He "came into the world to *save*" (1 Tim. 1:15, italics mine).

Illustration

History illustrates the saving power of a single name. The story is told of Croesus, the last king of Lydia, who had been defeated and sentenced to death by Cyrus II, the king of Persia. As he lay on the funeral pyre (the pile of wood on which a body is burned), Croesus called on the name of his friend Solon, who was widely known for his compassion. Cyrus asked the meaning of the cry, and on being told it was a cry for mercy, he had compassion on Croesus and released him. It has been said that he treated Croesus with respect and honor from that moment on.

In the third place, these words give us a revelation of the Savior's:

C. Nature

"Christ Jesus"; *Christ* reveals His divine nature, while *Jesus* reveals His human nature. In this blessed Savior, therefore, we have God and man. This great truth demonstrates the uniqueness of Christ. The apostle states, "For there is one God and one Mediator between God and men, the Man Christ Jesus" (1 Tim. 2:5). He alone can understand man, because He is Man of very man. He alone can undertake for man, because He is God of very God. Here then is the revealed Savior. In the revelation of His nativity, His name, and His nature, we see the Savior's advent and authority for the purpose of saving sinners.

Our text speaks further of our Savior:

II. The Redemption in the Savior

Paul declares, "Christ Jesus came into the world *to save sinners*" (1 Tim. 1:15, italics mine). In the redeeming work of Christ, Paul found and you and I can find pardon, power, and purpose:

A. *The Savior's Pardon*

"I obtained mercy," says the apostle, who was "formerly a blasphemer, a persecutor, and an insolent man" (1 Tim. 1:13). He revels in "the grace of our Lord [which] was exceedingly abundant" (v. 14). In it he found pardon for:

1. HIS SPIRITUAL SINS

He was "a blasphemer." He could say afterward, "I . . . thought I must do many things contrary to the name of Jesus" (Acts 26:9). "I . . . compelled them to blaspheme" (v. 11).

2. HIS SOCIAL SINS

He was "a persecutor." He says, "I persecuted the church of God beyond measure and tried to destroy it" (Gal. 1:13). He not only witnessed, but also approved of the murder of Stephen and thereafter he panted like a wild beast for the blood of the church.

3. His Selfish Sins

He was "an insolent man," or a "doer of outrage." He gave reign to his passions, until "sin, taking opportunity by the commandment, produced in [him] all manner of evil desire" (Rom. 7:8).

In spite of such a crime sheet, he "obtained mercy" from a pardoning Savior. Later he could write, "Having wiped out the handwriting of requirements that was against us, which was contrary to us. And He [the Savior] has taken it out of the way, having nailed it to the cross" (Col. 2:14). My friend, do you know this redemptive pardon? Have you ever had your spiritual, social, and selfish sins blotted out?

Illustration

A sick soldier, whose suffering was so great that he often wished he were dead, was asked about his soul. "Do you hope to escape everlasting pain?" He replied, "I am praying to God and striving to do my duty as well as I can." "What are you praying for?" he was asked. "For the forgiveness of my sins," he replied. "But if your wife were offering you a cup of tea she had lovingly prepared for you, what would be your response?" "To take it from her gratefully." The evangelist then said, "Since God is offering you pardon because of the Lord Jesus, what is your duty?" With much feeling and joyful faith, the soldier responded, "I ought to accept it!"[1]

B. The Savior's Power

Paul testified, "I thank Christ Jesus our Lord who has *enabled* me, because He counted me faithful, putting me into the ministry" (1 Tim. 1:12, italics mine). How often people say, "I would become a Christian, but I'm afraid I wouldn't be able to keep it up!" What an answer the apostle gives to this invention of the devil: I thank Christ Jesus our Lord, who has given me strength within to live as a faithful Christian.

C. The Savior's Purpose

Paul continues: "However, for this reason I obtained mercy, that in me first Jesus Christ might show all long-suffering, as a pattern to those who are going to believe on Him for everlasting life" (1 Tim. 1:16). There was a purpose for which and to which the Lord had saved him. God had a plan for Paul and, indeed, He has a plan for all who enter into Christ's redemptive purpose. It is written, "For we are His workmanship, created in Christ Jesus for good works, which God prepared beforehand that we should walk in them" (Eph. 2:10).

Tell me, have *you* found this redemptive pardon, power, and purpose for your life? If not, then you are missing the very object for which Christ Jesus came into the world. You might reply, "All this sounds too good to be true." Do not believe it! Paul presents not only the revelation of the Savior, and the redemption in the Savior, but also:

III. The Recommendation to the Savior

"This is a faithful saying and worthy of all acceptance" (1 Tim. 1:15). But how do you know, Paul? Because Christ Jesus came into the world to save sinners, of whom I am chief. I was a blasphemer, a persecutor, and an injurious sinner; but this matchless Savior saved me. So I recommend him to you.

A. Christ Jesus Is a Faithful Savior

This is a word to *the hesitating sinner.* Christ has been proved and found faithful by millions of men and women down through the centuries. Henry Alford has put it like this:

> Ten thousand times ten thousand
> In sparkling raiment bright,
> The armies of the ransomed saints
> Throng up the steeps of light:
> 'Tis finished, all is finished,
> Their fight with death and sin:
> Fling open wide the golden gates,
> And let the victors in.

B. Christ Jesus Is a Worthy Savior

This is a word to *the high-minded sinner.* He conde-scends to be your Savior, but He never apologizes.

C. Christ Jesus Is an Acceptable Savior

This is a word to *the halfhearted sinner.* He is worthy not only of universal acceptance, but of wholehearted acceptance. He is God's supreme lovegift.

> When I survey the wondrous cross,
> On which the Prince of glory died,
> My richest gain I count but loss,
> And pour contempt on all my pride.
>
> Were the whole realm of nature mine,
> That were a present far too small;
> Love so amazing, so divine,
> Demands my soul, my life, my all.

> Isaac Watts

Illustration

C. T. Studd, world-renowned cricketer and sacrificial phi-lanthropist, said: "If Jesus Christ be God and died for me, then no sacrifice can be too great for me to make for Him."[2]

Conclusion

The truth about the Savior of sinners is followed in our text by a doxology of honor and glory to the Lord Jesus, whom Paul calls "the King eternal, immortal, invisible, [the] God who alone is wise" (1 Tim. 1:17). The great preacher and theologian Jonathan Edwards was suddenly converted as by a flash of light in the moment he read this single verse. So in viewing the majesty and power of the Savior, each person should turn in faith to the Lord Jesus.

4

We Must Glory in the Cross

Galatians 6:11–18

> But God forbid that I should glory except in the cross of our Lord Jesus Christ, by whom the world has been crucified to me, and I to the world.
>
> Galatians 6:14

Introduction

Galatians was written to a group of churches in what is now known as Asia Minor. Paul's burden, among a number of other issues, was that they had so soon moved from the grace of Christ to another gospel. So he had to say to them in no uncertain terms: "O foolish Galatians! Who has bewitched you that you should not obey the truth. . . . Did you receive the Spirit by the works of the law, or by the hearing of faith? Are you so foolish? Having begun in the Spirit, are you now being made perfect by the flesh?" (Gal. 3:1–3). He has blazed out in that first chapter: "But even if we, or an angel from heaven, preach any other gospel to you than what we have preached to you, let him be accursed" (Gal. 1:8).

So he carries through his well-argued dissertation on the gospel of our Lord Jesus Christ, climaxing with those tremendous words of our text. The message for you and me is clear:

I. We Must Glory in the Person of the Cross

"But God forbid that I should glory except in the cross of our Lord Jesus Christ" (Gal. 6:14). There is a sense in which we can never know our Lord Jesus Christ without the cross. Liberals attempt to do that. And I am deeply concerned at the way the cross is being dodged by many evangelical preachers as well. The penal aspect of the death of the Lord Jesus Christ is the essence of the gospel. Paul says, "I declare to you the gospel which I preached to you, . . . by which also you are saved. . . . that Christ died for our sins according to the Scriptures, and that He was buried, and that He rose again the third day according to the Scriptures" (1 Cor. 15:1–4). Jesus had to die, for "without the shedding of blood there is no remission" for sins (Heb. 9:22). Three beams of light shine from that cross:

A. *Our Lord's Divine Sovereignty*

"But God forbid that I should glory except in the cross of our *Lord*." The lordship of Christ is an inherent quality of deity. Just as He manifested that Lordship during His life, so there was a special and peculiar manifestation of the glory of His divine sovereignty at Calvary. When Peter preached on the day of Pentecost, he used language that is quite amazing. Addressing those who crucified the Lord Jesus Christ, he says, "Him, being delivered by *the determined counsel and foreknowledge of God,* you have taken by lawless hands, have crucified, and put to death" (Acts 2:23, italics mine).

There was a sovereignty about His death, for He chose the *manner* of His death and unfolded it to His disciples: "The Son of Man must be delivered into the hands of sinful men, and be crucified" (Luke 24:7).

He knew the *motive* of His death. Jesus never ceased to be God of very God while Man of very man. He knew exactly why He was going to die. He said, "The Son of Man did not come to be served, but to serve, and to give His life a ransom for many" (Mark 10:45).

Unlike any other person before him, or since, He knew the *moment* of his death. Having accomplished the work that God gave him to do, he bowed his head and dismissed his spirit (John 19:30). The Greek word there is exactly the same as our Savior used when He set forth the terms of discipleship to a young man, "Foxes have holes and birds of the air have nests, but the Son of Man has nowhere *to lay His head*" (Luke 9:58, italics mine). When Jesus died, His head did not drop or droop for lack of His control. He deliberately set His head forward and dismissed His spirit. He knew that it was time to die.

Not only do we see His divine sovereignty manifested at Calvary, but we also see His divine saviorhood:

B. Our Lord's Divine Saviorhood

"But God forbid that I should glory except in the cross of our Lord *Jesus*." Paul states, "God . . . desires all men to be saved and to come to the knowledge of the truth. . . . who gave Himself a ransom for all" (1 Tim. 2:3–6). Jesus died to become your Savior. As the old hymn puts it:

> He died that we might be forgiven,
> He died to make us good,
> That we might go at last to heaven,
> Saved by His precious blood.
>
> Cecil Alexander

You would never know salvation from the penalty of sin, the power of sin, or, one day, from the very presence of sin, were it not for the fact that Jesus died at Calvary. His name is Jesus, "for He will save His people from their sins" (Matt. 1:21).

But look again. Not only do we see his divine sovereignty and His divine saviorhood, but we also see His divine sufficiency.

C. Our Lord's Divine Sufficiency

"But God forbid that I should glory except in the cross of our Lord Jesus *Christ.*" "Christ" is His official title and means "the anointed One." It has its roots in the Old Testament word *Messiah,* and in the New Testament word *Christos.* He is seen as the anointed Prophet, Priest, and King. Whenever we find the title "Christ," it always gathers up the concept of his sufficiency. That is why Paul tells us, "For in Him dwells all the fullness of the Godhead bodily" (Col. 2:9). If you want to learn something of divine sufficiency look at the cross. Peter sums it up in the following paragraph:

> For to this you were called, because Christ also suffered for us, leaving us an example, that you should follow His steps: "Who committed no sin, nor was guile found in His mouth"; who, when He was reviled, did not revile in return; when He suffered, He did not threaten, but committed Himself to Him who judges righteously; who Himself bore our sins in His own body on the tree, that we, having died to sins, might live for righteousness— by whose stripes you were healed.
>
> 1 Peter 2:21–24

Have you knelt at Calvary and said, "God forbid that I should glory, save in the cross of my Lord Jesus Christ?" So we must glory in the Person of the cross. Then:

II. We Must Glory in the Purpose of the Cross

"But God forbid that I should glory except in the cross of our Lord Jesus Christ, *by whom the world has been crucified to me*" (Gal. 6:14, italics mine).

If I were to ask why God sent His Son to the cross of Calvary, I wonder what answers I would get. Some would say that God is God and His righteousness had to be vindicated in a world where man had broken His law—and that would be true. Some would say that the reason for the cross is so that man can be redeemed and reconciled to God. Others would add that man might receive forgiveness and cleansing; and still others would indicate that on the basis of the cross, man may have the regeneration of the Holy Spirit. All those answers would be right.

But I believe it goes even further. God created man for fellowship. Reciprocal love is the supreme purpose of the universe. But when sin came into the world, that fellowship was broken, and God was robbed of the love for which He longed. God is all-sufficient in and of Himself but in His inscrutable wisdom He wanted to share that love with man and have that love reciprocated. As someone has said, "The greatest sin in all the universe is unrequited love." The world came between man and God and robbed God of the love that He should have from our hearts. When Paul says, "The world has been crucified to me," he is talking, first of all, about:

A. *The Termination of a False Love*

"The world has been crucified to me, and I to the world" (Gal. 6:14). What is this false love? the love of the world. John describes it to us as "the lust of the flesh, the lust of the eyes, and the pride of life" (1 John 2:16). It refers, first of all to:

1. A LOVE THAT IS SENSUOUS

"The lust of the flesh"; this is what is visualized on television, glamorized in Hollywood, and rationalized in so many hearts.

Illustration

Some time ago there was a TV special titled "Born Again," which documented the whole spectrum of evangelism, including the incentives of material and physical benefits. A well-known theologian was asked to comment. Though a liberal, he declared, "Give me the fire and brimstone. Give me the preaching of hell. Give me every type of evangelism that brings the fear of God on men rather than the slick kind of evangelism today that unites us to the very world from which we are supposed to be saved." And he gave two illustrations—the apostle Paul and Martin Luther. When these men were converted, each man turned from the very system with which he had formerly been associated.

The whole mood today is "Get with it. The more worldly you are, the more effective you are." It's a hellish lie! When we talk about the glory of the cross, we are talking about something that cuts right across the love of the world, a love that is sensuous.

The love of the world also refers to:

2. A Love That Is Covetous

"The lust of the eyes" brought Eve into trouble. Even Paul said, "I would not have known sin except through the law. For I would not have known covetousness unless the law had said, 'You shall not covet'" (Rom. 7:7). As the Spirit of God applied that truth to his heart, he was condemned.

The love of the world is a love that is sensuous and it is a love that is covetous. It is also:

3. A Love That Is Vacuous

"The pride of life"; it is vainglory—puffing ourselves up, seizing power and prominence. Is it any wonder that Paul says, "God forbid" (Gal. 6:14)?

But with the termination of a false love, there must be:

B. The Generation of a True Love

On the basis of Calvary, we can know the release of the Spirit in our lives, for "the love of God has been poured out in our hearts by the Holy Spirit who was given to us" (Rom. 5:5), and a new love is generated. Do you know where that love is demonstrated? First of all, in:

1. THE LOVE FOR OUR SAVIOR

"We love Him because He first loved us" (1 John 4:19). He becomes the very beloved of our hearts and holds an unrivaled place in our lives. He becomes the very rose of Sharon, the bright and morning star, the lily of the valley, and the lover of our souls.

That true love is not demonstrated only in the love for our Savior, but also in:

2. THE LOVE FOR OUR BROTHER

"We know that we have passed from death to life, because we love the brethren. He who does not love his brother abides in death" (1 John 3:14). When I think of the factions, the unforgivingness, the schisms within the Christian church today, I wonder how many people really know the glory of the cross. You see, when a person knows the glory of the cross, not only is false love terminated, but true love is generated—agape love for our Savior and for our brother and also for our neighbor:

3. THE LOVE FOR OUR NEIGHBOR

"'You shall love the LORD your God with all your heart, with all your soul, with all your strength, and with all your mind,' and 'your neighbor as yourself'" (Luke 10:27). That neighbor can be the sinner alongside of you in the office. He may be across the sea, of a different color or culture, but he is your neighbor. And if we know anything of the glory of the cross, the love that God wants to shed on a loveless world must be let loose. We must reach out to a lost world.

But let us go further:

III. We Must Glory in the Power of the Cross

"But God forbid that I should glory except in the cross of our Lord Jesus Christ, by whom the world has been crucified to me, *and I to the world*" (Gal. 6:14, italics mine). This text speaks of three crucifixions—the crucifixion of our Lord, the crucifixion of the world, and the crucifixion of ourselves. It is this third aspect that needs stressing.

When we really know something of the cross in our lives, we see not only the person, not only the purpose, but we experience the power of the cross, allowing us to face the world.

A. We Have Power to Face the World with Victory

"This is the victory that has overcome the world—our faith" (1 John 5:4). The apostle John is echoing the Lord Jesus when he said, "Be of good cheer, I have overcome the world" (John 16:33). Within that context he was referring to two things about the world, namely, persecution and tribulation.

Concerning *persecution in the world,* Jesus said, "These things I have spoken to you, that you should not be made to stumble. . . . the time is coming that whoever kills you will think that he offers God service" (John 16:1–2). When Christians are popular among "worldly" sinners, there is cause for concern. In these days of détente and compromise, we have to be very careful.

Illustration

Stephen Olford relates: Over recent decades in countries like Chad, Cambodia, Uganda, Angola, China, and Russia, there has been persecution. Festo Kivengere, a faithful Ugandan leader, said, "It is tragic. Three hundred thousand people have been massacred—many of them Christians, but," he added, "my heart rejoices because the church is growing as it has never grown. The church is giving as it has never given, and the church is singing, and they even have a kind of national anthem for the church of Jesus Christ in the face of martyrdom."

The power of the cross enables us to deal not only with persecution in the world, but also with *tribulation in the world.* "In the world you will have tribulation," said Jesus (John 16:33). But when we glory in the cross, there is victory as we face the world—whether it is in persecution or tribulation.

B. We Have Power to Face the World with Purity

James says, "Keep [yourselves] unspotted from the world" (James 1:27). The distinctive mark of the Lord Jesus throughout His earthly years was holiness. Even though He ate and drank with sinners and interacted to win them, He was "holy, harmless, undefiled, separate from sinners" (Heb. 7:26). And Paul says in Romans 1:4 that Jesus Christ was "declared to be the Son of God with power, according to the Spirit of holiness."

We live in a polluted, defiled, sin-laden atmosphere today, and yet God expects us to be holy in our spirits, souls, and *bodies.* Paul prays, "May your whole spirit, soul, and body be preserved blameless at the coming of our Lord Jesus Christ" (1 Thess. 5:23).

So the cross gives us power to face the world with victory and with purity.

C. We Have Power to Face the World with Constancy

"And the world is passing away, and the lust of it; but he who does the will of God abides forever" (1 John 2:17). Great changes are swiftly occurring in our day. The biggest cultural shock to missionaries today is not going into a foreign culture, but returning to their homeland and encountering worldliness and carnality in the home church that they never anticipated. In one denomination alone there are one thousand preachers a year who drop out of the ministry. They are breaking down under the pressures of our modern day. The old hymn says, "Change and decay in all around I see." But despite the changes, we can face this fading and failing world knowing that in doing the will of God, we shall abide forever!

Illustration

At the Milan Cathedral there are three doorways, each with a different inscription. Over the right-hand portal is a sculptured wreath of flowers with the motto: "All that pleases is but for a moment." Over the left-hand entrance are a cross and crown, under which are the words: "All that troubles is but for a moment." But over the central door there is a simple sentence: "Nothing is important save that which is eternal."

Stephen Olford relates: God used the lines of a simple couplet to bring me to kneel before the cross. At the time I was on my deathbed, with only two weeks to live. A letter from my father in Africa, written three months before (mail service was slow in those days), was placed on my bed. At the very heart of the letter were these words: "My son, this is of most importance:

'Only one life, 'twill soon be past,
Only what's done for Christ will last.'"

Up until that moment I had lived for the world instead of God. And I remember getting out of my bed and dropping on my knees (though I was not allowed to) and surrendering everything to Jesus Christ. Praise God, I was not only forgiven but healed!

Conclusion

What about you? The choice rests with you. The glory of the cross is the glory of His person, His purpose, and His power. Will you look at that cross and beyond it to Christ, and give your answer?

5

The Fate of Fruitlessness

Mark 11:12–14, 20–26

[Jesus] was hungry. And seeing from afar a fig tree having leaves, He went to see.... And when He came to it, He found nothing but leaves.... In response Jesus said to it, "Let no one eat fruit from you ever again."... Now in the morning, as they passed by, they saw the fig tree dried up from the roots. And Peter, remembering, said to Him, "Rabbi, look! The fig tree which You cursed has withered away." So Jesus answered and said to them, "Have faith in God."

Mark 11:12–14, 20–22

Introduction

This is the only miracle of judgment performed by our Lord Jesus Christ. It is significant that it comes at the end of His ministry. For three and a half years the Master had lived, taught, and worked to bring the Jewish nation to repentance and faith in God. But except for His immediate disciples and a circle of other faithful followers, His own people had rejected Him. "He came to His own, and His own did not receive Him" (John 1:11).

The events of Palm Sunday had demonstrated this fact in a most painful manner. In coming to Jerusalem He had had to face the shallow jubilation of the crowd, the solemn desolation of the city, and the shameful desecration of the temple. All this and more had brought Him to the point when He had to reject His own people. To announce this sad but decisive fact, Jesus enacted a parable, known to us today as the cursing of the barren fig tree.

As Lord of all the earth He had a perfect right to destroy the tree if only to fulfill His own holy purpose. To criticize what our Lord did is as ridiculous as it is to condemn a father for cutting down a Christmas tree for his family, or a botanist for plucking petals from a flower to instruct his pupils. True, this was an act of judgment, for God must judge fruitlessness wherever He finds it: in physical life, national life, personal life, or spiritual life. The fate of fruitlessness is based on:

I. The Master's Ruined Expectation

"And seeing from afar a fig tree having leaves, He went to see if perhaps He would find something on it" (Mark 11:13). There was every reason to expect fruit, for, if St. Jerome can be trusted, his writings prove that fig trees throughout Palestine could produce fruit any month of the year except January and February.

Illustration

The fig was a common and much esteemed food. There were three kinds: the early fig, which ripened after a mild winter at the end of June, and in Jerusalem still earlier; the summer fig, which ripened in August; the winter fig, which came to maturity only after the leaves were gone and would hang through a mild winter into the spring.

This last kind cannot be meant here, since a winter fig tree would probably have been robbed of its fruit long before Passover time. This was apparently a reference to very early spring figs. The extraordinary show of leaves so early gave

> promise of early figs, since on the fig tree, the blossom and fruit appear before the formation of the leaves. Thus it was the profusion of leaves that caused the Lord to expect to find figs on the tree.[1]

When Jesus looked up into the leafy tree, He found only leaves, a ruined expectation. He had come to His own people and lived, worked, and taught to bring them to repentance, regeneration, and righteousness. But He was disappointed. How long has Christ, by His Spirit, come to your life seeking fruit? Jesus was expecting the fruit of repentance:

A. Repentance

Indeed, John the Baptist had prepared the way for the world: "Therefore bear fruits worthy of repentance" (Matt. 3:8), or bring forth fruit commensurate with the amendment of your life. With all the preaching of the Master, the demonstration of His power, and the radiance of His holy life, the nation had refused to come to Him. Later He had to weep, "O Jerusalem, Jerusalem, the one who kills the prophets and stones those who are sent to her! How often I wanted to gather your children together, as a hen gathers her chicks under her wings, but you were not willing!" (Matt. 23:37).

The Lord Jesus came to that tree expecting not only the fruit of repentance, but also the fruit of regeneration:

B. Regeneration

He had preached the message of the new birth. He had not only addressed a brilliant theologian with the words, "You must be born again" (John 3:7), but preached life again and again. "You search the Scriptures, for in them you think you have eternal life; and these are they which testify of Me" (John 5:39). And further, "But you are not willing to come to Me" (v. 40). Has the Savior come to your life seeking the fruit of repentance and found nothing but leaves? Has he come to your life seeking the fruit of regeneration but found nothing but leaves?

Jesus also came seeking the fruit of righteousness:

C. Righteousness

He sought righteousness among his own people and said, "Unless your righteousness exceeds the righteousness of the scribes and Pharisees, you will by no means enter the kingdom of heaven" (Matt. 5:20). Paul has a glorious little phrase in the first chapter of Philippians when he talks about "being filled with the fruits of righteousness which are by Jesus Christ, to the glory and praise of God" (Phil. 1:11). Do you know what it is to rise in triumph, radiance, strength, and nobility by the power of that imputed and imparted righteousness through Jesus Christ to the glory of God? Is your life a life of righteousness, or has Jesus come to you again only to find nothing but leaves, a ruined expectation?

There is another reason why He cursed and condemned this tree. I believe it is summed up in these words:

II. The Master's Righteous Indignation

"My Spirit shall not strive with man forever" (Gen. 6:3). There must come a point when judgment falls, or else God ceases to be God and His holy, righteous judgments cease to be judgment at all. Man fills his cup of arrogance and rebellion and impenitence, and God must judge.

That is what happened in the days of our Savior, and that is what happens today. It is possible for men and women in America not to recognize the day of God's visitation, and for that day to come and go. Why did Jesus judge this fig tree in righteous indignation? For three reasons:

A. Promise without Performance

The leaves were there, the promise of fruit, and He was hungry but He found no fruit. This is true of thousands of religious people throughout America. The Savior had to point His finger at religious people and say, "Not everyone who says to Me, 'Lord, Lord,' shall enter the kingdom of heaven, but he who does the will of My Father in heaven" (Matt. 7:21). America is full of people who can use all the clichés of evangelical Christianity. They say, "Lord," but they do not perform. They do not obey Him as Lord.

Illustration

A Scottish minister tells of one of his parishioners who sang most piously:

> "Were the whole realm of nature mine,
> That were a present far too small,"

And all through the singing was fumbling in his pocket to find the smallest coin for the offering basket.[2]

A day is coming when judgment shall fall on all such people. Some of the most solemn words that I find in Scripture are in the Sermon on the Mount, "Many will say to Me in that day, 'Lord, Lord, have we not prophesied in Your name, cast out demons in Your name, and done many wonders in Your name?' And then I will declare to them, 'I never knew you; depart from Me, you who practice lawlessness!'" (Matt. 7:22–23). Do you remember the day when you bowed in some quiet place and gave the Lord the answer concerning the ministry or the mission field? Has your promise been without performance?

Jesus' righteous indignation was expressed not only because of the promise without performance, but also because of the:

B. Profession without Possession

The leaves were there and they could be seen from afar, but there was no fruit. Jesus said the same thing in other words when He looked into the eyes of the religious people and said, "These people draw near to Me with their mouth, and honor Me with their lips, but their heart is far from Me" (Matt. 15:8). They knew how to honor Him outwardly, the leaves were there, the ardor was there, but the hearts were empty.

Christendom throughout America today is symbolized in the old fig tree. There are hundreds of people who are carried along by the Holy Spirit, (Gr. *metochos,* going along with, as in Hebrews 6:4), influenced by the Spirit, but not indwelt by God the Holy Spirit. They have never been sealed for the day of redemption. They do not know the indwelling of the Spirit, and because of this, their profession does not matter.

But further, Jesus cursed the tree because of its:

C. Position without Permission

Here was a nation given a wonderful place, but now assuming that place without permission, for they were not fulfilling the first purpose for which God put them there. There is a very solemn verse in Matthew's gospel: "Every plant which My heavenly Father has not planted will be uprooted" (Matt. 15:13). And He goes on to say, speaking of religious people, "They are blind leaders of the blind. And if the blind leads the blind, both will fall into a ditch" (v. 14). There are offices, positions, responsibilities, and duties held by people in the churches of our land today for which there is no divine permission. It is like the fig tree of Luke 13:6–7. When the owner came to his vineyard and saw the tree had not yielded fruit for three years, he had it cut down.

Why should anyone serve in any given capacity if he or she does not belong there by divine permission? The votes of people and the instrumentalities that people use to get a man into position never constitute that God-given permission. This is where Christ from heaven as Judge of the church comes down among His candlesticks and takes a candlestick or an individual away. He must judge sin in the midst of His people. He must judge anything that is nothing but leaves. But He did not end the subject there.

Not only is a ruined expectation and a righteous indignation expressed by the Savior, but there is:

III. The Master's Ready Explanation

Mark listened carefully so that he could recall these words, "And Peter, remembering, said to Him, 'Rabbi, look! The fig tree which You cursed has withered away.' So Jesus answered and said to them, 'Have faith in God'" (11:21–22). Hudson Taylor used to translate this from his own Greek New Testament, "hold on to the faithfulness of God." And then the Lord continues,

> For assuredly, I say to you, whoever says to this mountain, "Be removed and be cast into the sea," and does not doubt in his heart, but believes that those things he says will come to pass, he will have whatever he says. Therefore I say to you, whatever things you ask when you pray, believe that you receive them, and you will have them. And whenever you stand praying, if you have anything against anyone, forgive him, that your Father in heaven may also forgive you your trespasses. But if you do not forgive, neither will your Father in heaven forgive your trespasses.
>
> Mark 11:23–26

Jesus is giving a ready explanation as to why He cursed that barren fig tree, which symbolized the nation of Israel and, by application, your life and mine. The only qualification for being spared by God is to produce the fruit of a living faith, which, by definition is:

A. A Believing Faith

This is a faith in God that allows no interference, a faith so great, yet simple and sincere, that it is prepared to say to God, "Remove this mountain and cast it into the midst of the sea" and believes that God can and will do it. For those who try to rationalize this passage and explain away this mountain as merely an abstract or a moral mountain, do so to have their own way. The only faith that justifies its validity is the faith that believes that there is nothing that God cannot do, for we read, "The just shall live by faith" (Hab. 2:4; Rom. 1:17; Heb. 10:38).

A living faith is not only a believing faith, it is:

B. A Receiving Faith

"Whatever things you ask when you pray, believe that you receive them, and you will have them." There are hundreds and hundreds of people who go on believing but never receiving. The person who really believes is the person who receives of all that God can give. Have you ever received; have you ever exercised receiving faith? Have you ever received God's Son?

Jesus adds a most amazing point. If the faith that justifies your existence before God is to be exercised right, it must not only be a believing faith, and a receiving faith, but:

C. A Forgiving Faith

An unforgiving spirit causes most problems in the world today and in your life and mine. The reason you have not come into the church of Jesus Christ is because there are certain things about the church that have irked you, and you have not been prepared to forgive.

Illustration

A lady in my church once said to me, "I cannot take this step of faith, believe that Jesus Christ is my Savior, and go through with Him, cost what it will, because I won't forgive." Resentment against God and His people so clogged her soul that she rejected the saving love of Christ.

A father said bitterly, "I am not going to trust Christ. I'll never forgive God for taking my boy in the war."

> A mother said, "I will not believe in God because my little baby died in my arms as I cried to God for the deliverance of that child."
>
> Somebody says, "I am not going to trust God because if God really cared, my business would not have gone into bankruptcy."
>
> "I won't trust God," says a young man, "because I asked Him to help me with my examination and I have failed."

Because of the unforgivingness of your spirit you are going to hell. A man who is going to go through with God has to stand in His presence in faith. It has to be a faith that believes, receives, and forgives.

Conclusion

You must judge whether you really are a barren fig tree waiting for the judgment stroke of God. It does not matter how many leaves you show, or what the profession, position, or promise of your life is. If you are fruitless before God, He must eventually confront your disappointing barrenness.

> The Master came to the fig tree
> And saw the foliage there
> Of thick and shady branches,
> To hungry eyes so fair.
> But He found that it was barren
> And bore no luscious fruit,
> For life was gone, and very soon
> 'Twas withered to the root.
>
> The Master came to the Temple
> And saw the worship there,
> The riches and the customs,
> To Jewish eyes so fair;
> But to Him 'twas all corruption,
> His house a den of thieves,
> And all its boasted glory
> Was fruitless, only leaves.

The Master to the assembly
Has come! What sees He here?
The busy round of service
And meetings held so dear.
But He sees the strife and divisions,
And His Holy Spirit grieves
To find that many efforts
Are fruitless, mostly leaves.[3]

What the Bible Says about Saving Faith

Romans 10:1–21

> So then faith comes by hearing, and hearing by the word of God.
>
> Romans 10:17

Introduction

Everyone lives by faith. Whether it is in personal, social, commercial, national, or international life, men and women have to exercise faith continually. In all these aspects of life, the object of faith always determines the quality of faith. Perhaps an illustration will help to illuminate this principle.

Illustration

Some botanists wished to collect some rare specimens of wildflowers, which grew on the side of a dangerous slope in the Scottish Highlands. They offered a local lad a liberal sum of money to descend by a rope and pick the flowers. The boy looked at the money, thought of the danger, and replied, "I will go if my father will hold the rope." The botanists agreed, and he went to fetch his father. On his return he handed the rope to his father, and with undaunted courage, allowed himself to be lowered over the precipice and to hang there while he filled his basket with the coveted flowers.

I can hear you saying, "What faith this boy had in his father." I agree with you. It was remarkable faith. But you know the strength of faith is always determined by the object in whom, or in which, that faith is reposed. If the object is worthy, then the faith is strong. On the other hand, if the object is unworthy, then the faith is weak.

When we come to the Christian message, we are exhorted to repose our faith in the Son of God and in the Word of God. The faith we employ is the same as that boy's faith, but the object of our faith is transcendentally different.

This act of believing God changes human faith into saving faith, natural faith into effectual faith. Such saving faith "comes by hearing, and hearing by the word of God."

I. The Advent of Saving Faith

"Faith comes by hearing, and hearing by the word of God" (Rom. 10:17). From the context you will notice that the advent of saving faith presupposes:

A. The Heralding of the Gospel

"Faith comes by hearing, and hearing by the word of God," or the gospel of Christ. Scholars are agreed that the phrase, "the word of God" should read, "the Word of Christ" or, more simply, "the gospel of Christ." Whether the gospel is conveyed through the printed page, communicated in personal conversation, or articulated from the pulpit or platform makes no difference so long as the gospel is preached. God has ordained that the gospel must be preached and that its sound should go into all the earth until all people in every generation shall have heard of the saving grace of Christ.

Illustration

Stephen Olford relates: I well remember the chief of a primitive tribe in Angola, Africa, who looked into my father's face and exclaimed after hearing the gospel for the first time, "Ngana, this is what we have been waiting for. Why has it taken you so long to reach us? Your message has taken away our fear and given us a faith."

The preaching of the gospel is a sheer necessity until time is no more. Every creature must hear the gospel through the foolishness of preaching. The apostle Paul sensed this burden when he said, "For if I preach the gospel, I have nothing to boast of, for necessity is laid upon me; yes, woe is me if I do not preach the gospel!" (1 Cor. 9:16).

B. The Hearing of the Gospel

"Faith comes by hearing." The gospel must not only be heralded; it must be heard. In his ministry, the Lord Jesus Christ was ever enforcing His teaching and preaching with the words, "He who has ears to hear, let him hear!" (Matt. 11:15). The reason for this is that only those who "hear the voice of the Son of God . . . will live" (John 5:25). The preaching of the gospel, therefore, calls for:

1. AN INTELLIGENT HEARING OF THE WORD OF GOD

"Faith comes by hearing." This point must be emphasized in view of the fact that there is so much *listening* without true *hearing* today. For example, there is what we might call:

• Nebulous Listening

This is the kind of listening that detects the sounds but does not distinguish the sense. Have you ever entered a room suddenly and asked a person who has been listening to the radio what the latest news is, only to get the rejoinder, "It is true I was listening, but somehow I did not hear what he said!"

• Credulous Listening

This is the foolish state of mind that will swallow anything. It is the hallmark of a foolish person, as opposed to a discerning person. How many there are today who gullibly believe anything and everything!

• Superstitious Listening

This is the kind of listening that is prejudiced or poisoned by fear, tradition, and even lies.

• Suspicious Listening

This is the mental outlook that doubts everything without reason or cause.

• Fictitious Listening

This is the mind-set of the imaginative person who invents the object of his trust. He puts his confidence in a feeble or nonexistent idol of his own making.

Now the preaching of the gospel sweeps away such superficial kinds of listening and claims the attention of the mind, the heart, and the will. It is recorded that when that wealthy woman Lydia listened to the apostle Paul, her heart was *opened* "to heed the things spoken" (Acts 16:14). Intelligent hearing leads to:

2. An Obedient Hearing of the Word of God

"Faith comes by hearing." Obedient hearing produces what the apostle calls the "obedience to the faith" (Rom. 1:5). Indeed, "faith without works is dead" (James 2:26). So we are exhorted to "be doers of the word, and not hearers only, deceiving yourselves" (James 1:22).

Illustration

Stephen Olford relates: On one occasion I visited a friend of mine who lived in a little attic room of a high building in the city of London. As I sat there talking with him, I ventured to ask him how he would escape from his room in the event of fire. I reminded him of the fact that there were no elevators and only one internal stairway.

Pointing to an object attached to his window, he said, "I have a fire escape ladder over there." With that, he proceeded to demonstrate the operation. Releasing two retaining straps, he unrolled the ladder out of his window and turned to me and said, "There, a perfect fire escape!" I replied, "Let me see you use it." At that point my friend's attitude changed! He was obviously not prepared to act on his knowledge of the fire escape and step out in faith! His faith was intelligent, but it certainly was not obedient.

In a similar way, no person can claim to have really heard the gospel who has not heeded it intelligently and obediently. You see, the gospel is never faithfully preached unless it claims a decisive verdict from the listener.

So the advent of faith comes through the heralding and the hearing of the gospel. But our text goes on to teach us something of faith's activity.

II. The Activity of Saving Faith

"Faith comes by hearing, and hearing by the word of God" (Rom. 10:17). In the context of this amazing verse, we are shown that the activity of saving faith is twofold:

A. It Levels Everyone to the Conditions of the Gospel

"'Whoever believes on Him will not be put to shame.' For there is no distinction between Jew and Greek, for the same Lord over all is rich to all who call upon Him" (Rom. 10:11–12). The advantages of intellect, opportunity, and substance do not operate in the sphere of faith. Faith places everyone in the same position as regards the grace of God. Faith minimizes man's merits while it magnifies God's mercy. And this is how it should be.

For if your salvation were based on your race, what would happen to some of the despised people of the world? If it were based on your riches, what would happen to those who are too poor to pay? If it were based on your rank, what would happen to those who cannot ascend to your social status? If it were based on your reading, what would happen to those who do not possess the academic qualifications that you have? If it were based on religion, what would happen to those whose religious ideas are diametrically opposed to yours? God sweeps all of these things aside and levels every man at the foot of the cross.

B. It Leads Everyone to the Christ of the Gospel

"Whoever calls upon the name of the LORD shall be saved" (Rom. 10:13). You cannot read the Scripture or hear the gospel preached without being led to the central fact and figure of the divine revelation, even our Lord Jesus Christ. He and He alone is the Savior of the world. "Nor is there salvation in any other, for there is no other name under heaven given among men by which we must be saved" (Acts 4:12).

Now there is one last thought, which must yet detain us:

III. The Affirmation of Saving Faith

"Faith comes by hearing, and hearing by the word of *God*" (Rom. 10:17, italics mine). The apostle Paul makes it plain that the affirmation of saving faith is confessing Christ as savior and sovereign.

A. The Confession of Christ as Savior

"With the mouth confession is made to salvation" (Rom. 10:10). As we have seen already, saving faith leads men and women to a personal Savior in Jesus Christ: a savior from the penalty and power of sin, and one day from the very presence of sin. This "salvation" involves "the death of the cross" (Phil. 2:8). Jesus paid our sin debt by shedding His most precious blood to set sinners free.

To call on Him, in the first instance, is to confess Him as Savior. Tell me, have you called on the name of the Lord? Have you openly affirmed your faith? Remember that it is with the mouth that confession is made for salvation.

This affirmation of saving faith is also:

B. The Confession of Christ as Sovereign

"If you confess with your mouth the Lord Jesus and believe in your heart that God raised Him from the dead, you will be saved" (Rom. 10:9). In another passage, Paul tells us that, "No one can say that Jesus is Lord except by the Holy Spirit" (1 Cor. 12:3). In other words, the affirmation of saving faith is the evidence that a man or woman has, in fact, accepted Christ as Savior and acknowledged Him as Lord.

The person who is unwilling to confess the lordship of Christ reveals that he or she is either unregenerate or apostate. This is why the first century preachers insisted on pressing home the sovereignty of Christ in every message that they delivered. How we need to return to such preaching today!

Without the lordship of Christ there is no life in Christ. Therefore Jesus Christ must be:

> Lord of ev'ry thought and action,
> Lord to send and Lord to stay;
> Lord in speaking, writing, giving,
> Lord of all things to obey;
> Lord of all there is of me,
> Now and evermore to be.
>
> E. H. Swinstead

Will you make this affirmation of your faith by confessing Christ as Savior and Sovereign of your life?

Conclusion

So we have seen that the advent of saving faith comes through the heralding and hearing of the gospel; the activity of faith levels all people to the conditions of the gospel, then leads them to the Christ of the gospel. The affirmation of faith confesses Christ as Savior and Lord. Have you exercised such faith in Christ? If not, will you do so now? Then respond with these words:

> My faith looks up to Thee,
> Thou Lamb of Calvary,
>   Savior divine!
> Now hear me while I pray,
> Take all my guilt away,
> O let me from this day
>   Be wholly Thine!

Ray Palmer

The Person Whom God Accepts

Luke 18:9–14

I tell you, this man [the tax collector] went down to his house justified rather than the other [the Pharisee]; for everyone who exalts himself will be abased, and he who humbles himself will be exalted.

Luke 18:14

Introduction

Jesus had been discoursing on prayer and, therefore, on a person's acceptability before God. And knowing the human heart, he anticipated the question that would inevitably arise in his hearers' minds: Who is the person whom God accepts? That question still needs urgent answering. For if ever there was a time when society as a whole talked so much about moral conduct, it is today. In fact people are more agreed on the need of morality than on the need for religion! The tragedy of it is that with all this interest in morality, men and women have ignored or neglected what God has to say on the matter; and morality has degenerated into self-trust and self-righteousness.

The Lord Jesus summed up this moral bankruptcy when he addressed those "who trusted in themselves that they were righteous, and despised others" (Luke 18:9). Then to determine the person whom God accepts, Jesus proceeded to tell a most revealing parable. He pictured two men going up into the temple to pray and then he disclosed how they appeared before God when shown up in the holy light of the divine presence. And then with dramatic and solemn vividness, He explained why God had to reject one man while He accepted the other. Let us first look at:

I. The Person Whom God Rejects

"For everyone who exalts himself will be abased" (Luke 18:14). It is quite clear from the story that this man was outstanding for his human morality. Consider three qualifications for this:

A. His Good Character

He was "a Pharisee" (Luke 18:10). A man had to have a good moral character to be a Pharisee. He had to become a member of an exclusive sect that prided itself on a high morality. You will remember that, as a Jew and as one boasting in the flesh, Paul gloried in the fact that he was a Pharisee. He said, "If anyone else thinks he may have confidence in the flesh, I more so: circumcised the eighth day, of the stock of Israel, of the tribe of Benjamin, a Hebrew of the Hebrews; concerning the law, a Pharisee" (Phil. 3:4–5). So it seems evident that this man in the parable was known for his good character.

Another qualification for his morality was:

B. *His Good Conduct*

His moral conduct is suggested by his prayer, "God, I thank You that I am not like other men—extortioners, unjust, adulterers, or even as this tax collector" (Luke 18:11). Though it sounds like pride, it is reasonable to believe that this soliloquy was factual and true. Without doubt, the Pharisee was genuinely thankful that he was not:

1. AN EXTORTIONER

The word denotes one who plunders, spoils, or robs. In one place it is translated "ravening" to describe the ruthless and vicious attack of hungry wolves. It is reasonable to believe, therefore, that the Pharisee was thankful that he was not an extortioner.

2. AN UNJUST PERSON

Unjust means "not in conformity with the right." The expression is used of the unjust judge in this same chapter, "who did not fear God nor regard man" (Luke 18:2). It signifies the characteristic outlook of the man or woman who refuses to accept any standard of morality whatsoever. It is reasonable to believe, therefore, that the Pharisee was thankful that he was not unjust.

3. AN ADULTERER

An adulterer is the person who has sexual intercourse with the spouse of another, sinking low enough to exploit the sacred union of marriage. It is reasonable to believe, therefore, that the Pharisee was thankful that he was not an adulterer.

4. A TAX COLLECTOR

A tax collector was a Jew who had sold his patriotic loyalties for the sake of making money. For this cause the tax collector was bitterly hated by the orthodox Jew and, in particular, by the Pharisees. It is reasonable to believe, therefore, that the Pharisee was thankful that he was not a tax collector.

We may justly conclude, then, that the Pharisee was good in conduct.

The third qualification for his morality was:

C. His Good Convictions

These were not only good, but also costly. Listen to them: "I fast twice a week; I give tithes of all that I possess" (Luke 18:12). His good convictions involved:

1. FASTING

"I fast twice a week." In the Law, God appointed but one fast day in the year. This was the Day of Atonement, when every Jew would cease from work and deny himself food so that he might afflict his soul and commemorate God's great deliverance out of Egypt (Num. 29:7).

But for this Pharisee, fasting once a year was not sufficient. He made this principle work twice a week, or 104 times a year! Would *you* allow your morality to carry you that far?

And then there was the:

2. TITHING

"I give tithes of all that I possess." The Law commanded that every Jew should tithe of the fruits of the field and of the increase of cattle (Lev. 27:30–32). But again, this was not sufficient for this man. He made the principle of tithing affect everything that he acquired.

Tell me, could *you* match this man's conscientious convictions? Whatever your answer, you will have to admit that this man's morality was of a very high order. And yet he was not accepted by God! Jesus tells us that he was not justified or made to appear before God in a favorable light!

The reason for this man's rejection is that he trusted in his OWN morality and righteousness for his acceptance before God. And because he made his good character, his good conduct, and his good convictions the ground of his justification before God, he was categorically rejected! Well did Isaiah declare hundreds of years before, "But we are all like an unclean thing, and all our righteousnesses are like filthy rags" (Isa. 64:6).

Now look at the second man:

II. The Person Whom God Accepts

"This man went down to his house justified" (Luke 18:14). We have only to glance at this man to recognize that he was sadly lacking in morality. Consider briefly:

A. His Bad Character

We read that he was "a tax collector" (Luke 18:10). As we have observed already, this man, although a Jew, was a bad character. Most tax collectors were, and there is no reason to believe that this man was any exception. He had bartered away all his loyalties and, therefore, deserved to be despised.

B. His Bad Conduct

He called himself "a sinner" (Luke 18:13), and without doubt this was a correct summing up of himself.

C. His Bad Convictions

His convictions must have been bad. If they were anything like the convictions held by the tax collector Zacchaeus, then they would be both unscrupulous and unprincipled (see Luke 19:1–10).

So, judged from every point of view, the tax collector was a man of very low, or no, morality. And yet God accepted him! In fact Jesus, commenting on the story, says, "This man went down to his house justified."

D. His Right Coming

The reason for this man's acceptance was not because of his badness, for the Savior certainly does not speak lightly of his sin. The reason for his acceptance is that this man came to God in the *only way* that God has prescribed for good and bad, rich and poor, young and old, illiterate and educated. Here is the way:

1. HE CAME WITH THE RIGHT SELFLESSNESS

"God be merciful to me a sinner!" (Luke 18:13). By the very use of the emphatic article *the* in the Greek, he narrowed himself down to the only sinner in the world. And, indeed, there is no other way to come to God.

Whatever your character, conduct, or convictions, you are still a sinner before God, and the acknowledgment of that fact is the first step into God's favor. It will smash your pride, it will test your courage, but it will save your soul.

Illustration

Stephen Olford relates: A number of years ago, I was conducting a crusade in Bournemouth, England. For our Sunday night meetings, we used the Boscombe Hippodrome. God was graciously with us, and great numbers were seeking the Savior. Particularly was this so on the evening I have in mind. In fact there were not enough counselors to meet the demand of seeking men and women. So I beckoned to my side a gentleman who was attired in clerical clothes. As he came forward, he whispered, "I am one of the seekers; I want a word with you as soon as you are free."

Later I discovered that this dear man had studied theology at Cambridge, completed five years curacy in England, and five years missionary work in Africa; but he was not saved! Not until that night, in the Boscombe Hippodrome, had he come to realize that "all his righteousnesses were as filthy rags," and that there was no other way to come to Jesus than as an unworthy bankrupt sinner. Thank God, he came that way and left rejoicing in Christ and His righteousness and life!

2. HE CAME WITH THE RIGHT SACRIFICE

"God be merciful to me a sinner!" He had no sacrifice of his own but with humble and holy boldness, he looked at the sacrifice that was being offered at that very hour in the temple and, claiming the lamb as his sin-bearer, he cried, "God be merciful to me a sinner!" Or more literally, "God be unto me, as when you look on atoning blood."

Illustration

It has been pointed out that this tax collector sent the shortest telegram to heaven reading:

> Address—"God"
> Message—"Have mercy on me"
> Signature—"The sinner"

In the language of the old hymn, the publican in effect prayed:

> Nothing in my hand I bring,
> Simply to Thy cross I cling;
> Naked, come to Thee for dress,
> Helpless, look to Thee for grace;
> Foul, I to the fountain fly,
> Wash me, Savior, or I die!
>
> Augustus M. Toplady

The way of the cross is still God's way of salvation. No other sacrifice will avail.

3. HE CAME WITH THE RIGHT SURRENDER

Smiting himself on his breast in utter brokenness, he dared to link himself with God: *"God* be merciful to *me"*; GOD—ME, and nothing but mercy between.

In all the virtue of the blood sacrifice, he surrendered himself by faith to God. And Jesus declared, "This man went down to his house justified"; or just as if he had never sinned. If you would be justified and accepted before a Holy God, you must come the same way.

Conclusion

So we have considered the person whom God rejects and we have observed the person whom God accepts. Which of these people represents you? I urge you to repent of your self-trust and self-righteousness; bring to God the right selflessness, the right sacrifice, and the right surrender; and humbly pray:

> Just as I am, without one plea,
> But that Thy blood was shed for me,
> And that Thou bidd'st me come to Thee,
> O Lamb of God, I come! I come!
>
> Charlotte Elliott

Spiritual Security

John 10:14–18, 26–30

> My sheep hear My voice, and I know them, and they follow Me. And I give them eternal life, and they shall never perish; neither shall anyone snatch them out of My hand. My Father, who has given them to Me, is greater than all; and no one is able to snatch them out of My Father's hand.
>
> John 10:27–29

Introduction

Psychologists tell us that one of the strongest instincts in the being of man is that of self-preservation. Wherever people are found on the face of the earth they are afraid of insecurity. Talk to any reasonable man or woman and he or she will share with you a concern for personal security, for social security, and even for national security. Indeed, much of our modern life is made up of insuring ourselves against poverty, sickness, and death.

There is another dimension of security to which many people give very little attention. It is that of eternal, or spiritual security. The Bible speaks of this again and again throughout its progressive revelation. Paul spoke of it when he said, "I know whom I have believed and am persuaded that He is able to keep what I have committed to Him until that Day" (2 Tim. 1:12). But our Lord Jesus Christ spoke the greatest statement that was ever made on the subject when he said,

> My sheep hear My voice, and I know them, and they fol-
> low Me. And I give them eternal life, and *they shall never*
> *perish; neither shall anyone snatch them out of My hand.*
> *My Father, who has given them to Me, is greater than all;*
> *and no one is able to snatch them out of My Father's hand.*
>
> John 10:27–29 (italics mine)

Tell me, do you know anything about this spiritual security in your life? Remember that personal, social, and national securities are only for time, but spiritual security is for time and eternity. In this glorious utterance of the Master, we have the offer of security to all who will fulfill the condition. This eternal security is based on:

I. A Divine Relationship

Jesus said, "I give *them* [my sheep] eternal life" (10:28). When the Savior specifically underscored the words "them" [my sheep] and "eternal life," He was presupposing a divine relationship; and because a divine relationship, it is described in this passage as:

A. A Living Relationship

"I give them eternal life" (10:28). The gospel of Jesus Christ is the gospel of eternal life. It is for this very purpose that the Savior came into the world. As we read in this very context, He could look into the faces of men and women, like you and me, and say, "I have come that they may have life, and that they may have it more abundantly" (10:10).

And John, in his epistle, reminds us that, "And this is the testimony: that God has given us eternal life, and this life is in His Son. He who has the Son has life; he who does not have the Son of God does not have life" (1 John 5:11–12).

And so we see that this divine relationship involves a living union with Jesus Christ. As the Lord Jesus is received into the heart and life by a personal faith, a living relationship is established that no devil in hell, no man on earth, and no angel in heaven can ever dissolve.

Do you share that life? Can you claim that the miracle has taken place, and that none other than the Son of God indwells you? I want you to notice, in the next place, that this divine relationship is:

B. A Lasting Relationship

"I give them eternal life, and they shall never perish" (10:28). There are two precious thoughts in this statement that we must consider carefully. The first concerns the word *eternal.* The term denotes not only quality of life, but also a quantity of life.

In quality, this eternal life is part of the very nature of God. By receiving eternal life we become "partakers of the divine nature" (2 Peter 1:4). But this life is also enduring and endless. The mind begins to reel when we try to think of the lastingness of the life that Jesus gives.

Illustration

Stephen Olford relates: I remember talking to my son, Jonathan, after he had received Christ into his life. I asked him if he were sure that he had received eternal life, and he answered, "Yes." Then I asked him how long the life would last, and he replied, "Forever." But I insisted further, "How long is forever?" to which he had no answer. So I proceeded to illustrate, as simply as possible, how we might conceive of everlasting life.

I said, "Think of all the leaves on every tree in all the world. Count them all up and multiply them by a billion. Then turn to the sand on the seashores all over the globe. Number every single grain and then multiply that number by a billion. When you have done that, try to calculate every drop of water in every river, and every ocean, and multiply that by a billion. That might illustrate eternal life."

His only remark was "That's a *long* time."

This lasting relationship is also strengthened by the second thought: "I give them eternal life, and they shall never perish" (10:28). In Greek that one sentence has a double negative, which is the strongest possible positive you can find in the Bible. The word *perish* is one of the most solemn words we find in the Scriptures. It carries the idea of ruination and purposelessness. A person who perishes not only deteriorates, but fails to fulfill the purpose for which he was created. This can happen in time and in eternity, but through a living relationship to Jesus Christ, we cease to perish and we enter into the fullness of eternal life.

What a wonderful sense of security is engendered in the human heart when we think of this living and lasting relationship to Jesus Christ!

Observe further that this eternal security is based on:

II. A Divine Reality

"My sheep hear My voice, and I know them, and they follow Me" (10:27). Jesus teaches us in these words that the reliability of eternal security is contingent on:

A. *The Authority of His Word*

"My sheep hear My voice" (10:27). Whenever the Savior opened His mouth, Scribes, Pharisees, men, and women were astonished at His doctrine because He spoke as one having authority (Mark 1:22). We can therefore rely on what He has to say about our eternal security. He declared, "Heaven and earth will pass away, but My words will by no means pass away" (Matt. 24:35). And again, "The Scripture cannot be broken" (John 10:35). And His message to your heart and mine is simply this, "My sheep hear My voice, and I know them, and they follow Me. And I give them eternal life, and they shall never perish" (10:27–28).

What greater reliability can we have than the authority of His word? But in addition to this, there is:

B. The Finality of His Work

"My sheep hear my voice, and I know them, and they follow Me" (10:27). In that phrase, "I know them," is gathered up the redemptive act by which he has made possible the salvation of every believing man or woman. He says,

> I am the good shepherd; and I know My sheep, and am known by My own. As the Father knows Me, even so I know the Father; and *I lay down My life for the sheep.* And other sheep I have which are not of this fold; them also I must bring, and they will hear My voice; and there will be one flock and one shepherd. Therefore My Father loves Me, because I lay down My life that I may take it again. No one takes it from Me, but I lay it down of Myself. I have power to lay it down, and I have power to take it again. This command I have received from My Father.
>
> John 10:14–18 (italics mine)

To doubt the offer of eternal security is to cast a serious reflection on the redemptive work of Jesus Christ. The hymn writer says it best:

> He died that we might be forgiven,
> He died to make us good,
> *That we might go at last to heaven,*
> *Saved by His precious blood.*
>
> Cecil F. Alexander (italics mine)

So we see that we can be certain of eternal security here and now because of the divine reliability of the word of

Christ and the work of Christ. But there is further thought that must engage our attention. It is simply this, that the offer of eternal security is based on:

III. A Divine Reassurance

"I give them eternal life, and they shall never perish; neither shall anyone snatch them out of My hand. My Father, who has given them to Me, is greater than all; and no one is able to snatch them out of My Father's hand" (10:28–29). You will notice that two hands are referred to in these verses. The one is the Savior's hand, and the other is the Father's hand. How completely reassuring it is, that once we become related to the Son of God, we are kept not only by the hand of our wonderful Shepherd, but also by the hand of our Heavenly Father. Let us examine, for a moment, the significance of these two hands. The first one represents:

A. The Savior's Hand of Saving Grace

"I give them eternal life, and they shall never perish; neither shall anyone snatch them out of My hand" (10:28). This is the pierced hand that has been stretched forth to lay hold of us in saving grace.

Illustration

Holman Hunt has beautifully depicted this aspect of the saving grace of Jesus. In a painting that I wish I could display before you now, the Good Shepherd is seen bending over a precipitous rock in order to lift the lost and wounded sheep from imminent danger and death. As you examine the picture, you can see the marks on his hands and feet from the thorns and briars. Love and tenderness are written all over his face. But the supreme message of the painting is that of the firm grip of the Shepherd's saving hand. Here is security indeed!

The story is told of a famous guide who had led thousands of tourists up the slippery slopes of the Swiss Alps. His climbing days were over, and his friends and admirers sought to do him honor by making him a presentation. After the speeches were over, the old man opened his hand to receive the gift, and anyone watching carefully could see those gnarled but strong hands of the old Swiss climber. Pointing to them, the mayor of the town declared, "Here are hands that have never lost a man."

My dear friend, I want to draw your attention to my Savior, who stands unseen to natural eyes, but very real to faith. As I point to those wounded hands, outstretched to save you, I want to remind you that here are the hands that have never lost a man. Herein is the divine reassurance of eternal security.

In closing, will you please observe that the second hand in our verse represents:

B. The Father's Hand of Sovereign Choice

"My Father, who has given them to Me, is greater than all; and no one is able to snatch them out of My Father's hand. I and my Father are one" (10:27–29). Here is a glorious fact. Long before the worlds were propelled into orbit and the universe was established by an act of divine will, God, in sovereign grace, chose everyone who would respond to the call of the Shepherd's voice.

Paul puts it succinctly when he says, "Blessed be the God and Father of our Lord Jesus Christ, who has blessed us with every spiritual blessing in the heavenly places in Christ, just as He *chose* us in Him before the foundation of the world, that we should be holy and without blame before Him in love" (Eph. 1:3–4). If God in His foreknowledge has laid His hand on me, can I have any doubt whatsoever about eternal security? The answer, of course, is a thousand times no!

So we have the hand of saving grace as well as the hand of sovereign choice. How completely reassuring! Do you know this eternal security? Remember that it is based on a divine relationship, a divine reliability, and a divine reassurance. This eternal security is offered to you *now* in Jesus Christ. To receive Him is to share His life, indeed, to be partaker of the divine nature. When the Savior's hand *and* the Father's hand close on you, no one is able to pluck you out of that secure and safe grasp.

Illustration

Stephen Olford relates: I remember the evangelist, Tom Rees, telling me of an occasion when he led a dear lad from the slums of London to a saving experience of Jesus Christ. The time came for the boy to return to his difficult home and surroundings. To give the boy some reassurance, the evangelist read the verses we have just been considering and explained something of the meaning of that safe hand of Jesus Christ. "But," remarked the boy with typical wit, "supposing I slip through his fingers?" "Ah, but that is impossible," said Tom Rees, "for when the Savior laid hold of you, you became one of his fingers!"

Conclusion

Here, then, is the offer of eternal security for you today. Will you receive Christ and enter into the joy of this living and lasting relationship? So I urge you in the Savior's name:

> Just now, your doubtings give o'er;
> Just now, reject him no more;
> Just now, throw open the door;
> Let Jesus come into your heart.
>
> Anonymous

Is There a Heaven to Gain?

John 14:1–6

Let not your heart be troubled; you believe in God, believe also in Me. In My Father's house are many mansions. . . . I go to prepare a place for you. . . . I will come again and receive you to Myself. . . .

I am the way, the truth, and the life. No one comes to the Father, except through Me.

John 14:1–3, 6

Introduction

Man is instinctively inquisitive about the future. With irrepressible longing he craves knowledge not only of tomorrow, but also of the life that lies beyond time's allotted span. Even the preoccupations of a materialistic age and the sarcastic protests of intellectual superiors do not seem to affect man's hope of heaven. He is convinced that if there is a heaven to gain, then there must be an assurance about the loved ones who have passed on. If there is a heaven to gain, then there must be a prospect for the Christian. He is convinced that if there is a heaven to gain, then there must be a purpose in living for God while here on earth. No doubt this is why Thomas Carlyle once said,

"He who has no vision of eternity will never get a true hold of time." So it is with some justification that I call your attention to the passage before us, and ask you to notice:

I. The Certainty of Heaven

"Let not your heart be troubled; you believe in God, believe also in Me" (John 14:1). If you will examine these words in their context and in light of other Scriptures, you will find that they teach that the certainty of heaven is:

A. Implicit in the Need of Man

"Let not your heart be troubled." The heart trouble that the Savior speaks about here is homesickness. The Lord Jesus had been telling the disciples, "I shall be with you a little while longer" (John 13:33), and the thought of His departure had made their hearts sink. They just could not imagine what life without Him would be like. He was their heaven, for "where Jesus is, 'tis heaven there."

These men were witnessing to the fact that heaven alone could satisfy their longing soul. And so it has always been. Man was made for heaven and will never rest until he finds his rest in the Christ of heaven. Thousands on thousands have expressed this restlessness or homesickness in many ways, but none has ever risen to the simplicity and certainty of the apostle Paul. Listen to his words, "For to me, to live is Christ, and to die is gain" (Phil. 1:21). "For I am hard pressed between the two, having a desire to depart and be with Christ, which is far better" (v. 23).

Most of us find it very difficult to want "heaven" at all—except in so far as "heaven" means meeting again our friends who have died. One reason for this difficulty is that we have not been trained. Our whole education tends to fix our minds on this world. Another reason is that when the real want for heaven is present in us, we do not recognize it. If people really learned to look into their own heart, they would know that they do want, and want acutely, something that cannot be found in this world. There are all sorts of things in this world that offer to give you "heaven," but they never do.[1]

The certainty of heaven is implicit in the need of man. That certainty of heaven is also:

B. Inherent in the Fact of God

"You believe in God," says Christ, "believe also in Me." In effect, the Lord Jesus was saying, belief in God means belief in Me, and belief in Me means belief in heaven. Speaking as a Son over the Father's house (Heb. 3:6), He surely could talk with authority on the certainty of heaven. So He adds, "If it were not so [if heaven were not a certainty], I would have told you" (John 14:2).

Remember, also, that the Lord Jesus was speaking those words in the shadow of the cross. What weight, then, would His teaching have carried if death were the end? No, Jesus saw heaven through the gates of death and, therefore, steadfastly set His face to lead the way to the glory land, leaving us this assurance: "Where I am, there you may be also" (v. 3).

Illustration

Billy Graham has said, "I believe that out there in space where there are one thousand million galaxies, each a hundred thousand light years or more in diameter, God can find some place to put us in heaven. I'm not worried about where it is. I know it is going to be where Jesus is."[2]

So we see that the certainty of heaven is not only implicit in the need of man, but also inherent in the fact of God.

II. The Concept of Heaven

"In My Father's house are many mansions" (John 14:2). What a glimpse of heaven in a single phrase! "Home" is one of the tenderest words in our English tongue, and I know why! It is the word that best describes heaven.

A. *Home Is the Place of Reunion*

That is just what heaven is going to mean. For next to the unutterable joy of seeing our Savior, heaven is going to include the happy reunion with, and the recognition of, loved ones and friends who have gone before.

Paul sums up the anticipation of reunion and recognition in heaven in words that were first addressed to his precious converts at Thessalonica, "For what is our hope, or joy, or crown of rejoicing? Is it not even *you* in the presence of our Lord Jesus Christ at His coming?" (1 Thess. 2:19, italics mine). Someone once asked George Macdonald the question, "Shall we know one another in heaven?" His pertinent reply was, "Shall we be greater fools in paradise than we are here?"

B. *Home Is the Place of Restfulness*

This will not mean inertia or inactivity, but the blessed and eternal:

1. REST FROM SIN

"But there shall by no means enter it [heaven] anything that defiles" (Rev. 21:27).

2. REST FROM SORROW

"And God will wipe away every tear from their eyes; there shall be no more . . . sorrow" (Rev. 21:4).

3. REST FROM SEPARATION

"There shall be no more death" (Rev. 21:4).

4. REST FROM STARVATION

"They shall neither hunger anymore nor thirst anymore" (Rev. 7:16).

5. REST FROM SHADOW

"And there shall be no night there" (Rev. 22:5).

Illustration

The story is told of the great Richard Baxter, author of the *Saint's Everlasting Rest*, that as he lay dying, he was heard to whisper in response to an inquiry as to how he felt, "I am almost well." For him, entry into heaven meant the saint's everlasting rest.

How true are those words written to the Hebrew believers long ago, "There remains therefore a rest for the people of God" (Heb. 4:9).

C. Home Is the Place of Rejoicing

Someone has called heaven the place of laughter, and so it is, for remember that heaven is the place where there are thousands of little children; and where children are there is laughter. But heaven is even more than laughter. We are told that for the believer, heaven is the place of "exceeding joy" (Jude 24).

What a home heaven is! Paul described departure for heaven as, "Absent from the body . . . present with the Lord" (2 Cor. 5:8).

Look again at our Scripture text and learn of:

III. The Completeness of Heaven

"I go to prepare a place for you" (John 14:2). A little reflection makes it clear that the preparations for heaven had to do with:

A. The Completing of Introductions in Heaven

When Jesus said, "I go to prepare a place for you," He had before Him the infinite cost of introducing sinful men and women to His Father, God. Such introductions incurred the price of blood.

By virtue of His own blood He entered "into heaven itself, now to appear in the presence of God for us" (Heb.

9:24). Thank God that the introductions have been completed, for all whose names are written in the Lamb's Book of Life! (Luke 10:20; Phil. 4:3; Heb. 12:23).

The preparations for heaven also had to do with:

B. The Completing of Reservations in Heaven

"I go to prepare a place for you" (John 14:2). For every redeemed soul, there is room in heaven. It is a place of extensive mansions and therefore it has room for all.

> There's a land that is fairer than day,
> And by faith we can see it afar;
> For the Father waits over the way,
> To prepare us a dwelling place there.
>
> S. F. Bennet

The preparations for heaven further had to do with:

C. The Completing of Occupations in Heaven

"I go to prepare a *place for you.*" Included in that promise are the occupations for man in his tripartite completeness:

1. FOR HIS RELEASED SPIRIT

The believer will enjoy unhindered worship "in spirit and truth" (John 4:23).

2. FOR HIS RAPTURED SOUL

The believer will enjoy unlimited knowledge, for what is eternal life but to know God and Jesus Christ? (John 17:3). Then will the believer know even as he is known (1 Cor. 13:12).

3. FOR HIS REDEEMED BODY

The believer will enjoy unfettered service. For it is written, "His servants shall serve Him" (Rev. 22:3). Such service will include sharing in the governmen-

tal judgment of the world and of angels: "Do you not
know that the saints will judge the world? . . . Do you
not know that we shall judge angels?" (1 Cor. 6:2–3).

So we see something of the completeness of heaven.
Then in the verses before us, Jesus further suggests:

IV. The Community of Heaven

"I will come again and receive you to Myself; that where
I am, there you may be also" (John 14:3). When the Savior
says "I," He speaks representatively of heaven; for when you
compare this statement with what is revealed elsewhere,
you discover that the community of heaven is composed
of:

A. The Father

Indeed, it is the "Father's house" (John 14:2).

B. The Son

"No one has ascended to heaven but He who came
down from heaven, that is, the Son of Man who is in
heaven" (John 3:13).

C. The Spirit

For John said, "I saw the Spirit descending from
heaven like a dove" (John 1:32).

D. The Angels

Speaking of heaven, the writer to the Hebrews declares,
"You have come to Mount Zion and to the city of the living God, the heavenly Jerusalem, to an innumerable company of angels" (Heb. 12:22).

E. The Saints

When John was permitted in vision to look into
heaven, he beheld "a great multitude which no one could

number, of all the nations, tribes, peoples, and tongues" (Rev. 7:9).

> Friends will be there I have loved long ago;
> Joy like a river around me will flow;
> Yet, just a smile from my Savior, I know,
> Will through the ages be glory for me.
>
> Charles H. Gabriel

In conclusion, see in the passage under consideration:

V. The Commendation of Heaven

"I am the way, the truth, and the life. No one comes to the Father except through Me" (John 14:6). Such a glimpse of heaven had called forth the most natural and crucial question from Thomas: "Lord, we do not know where you are going, and how can we know the way?" (v. 5). In reply, the Savior offers Himself as being the three indispensable requirements for an entrance into heaven:

A. The Way *to Escort Us to Heaven*

Christ is not only the path, but also the *guide* to the realms of bliss. Without Him we are most certainly lost. He says, "No one comes to the Father except through Me" (John 14:6).

Illustration

W. E. Vine informs us that the Greek word for "the Way," as applied to Christ, signified "the means of access." Only Christ gives us access to the Father and the Father's house. Let me illustrate this.

Stephen Olford relates: One of the most frightening and frustrating experiences of my life was to be put under house arrest because my American visa was challenged on entry to a country at war. The missionary who came to meet me tried his best to resolve the situation, but all his efforts were in vain. As I bowed in prayer, the thought occurred to me that my British passport might work! I asked the official in charge to phone the British Embassy and connect me to the ambassador. It was a Saturday afternoon and offices like this were normally closed. But in God's providence, he got through and handed me the phone. I introduced myself, explained my predicament, and gave him my passport number and relevant details. He said, "Hand the phone over to the official." In minutes I was a free man! With profuse apologies the official escorted me to my waiting car. The ambassador was my "means of access" to my desired destination. Jesus is our "means of access" to the Father's house!

Have you met this heavenly guide and friend?

The second essential that our Savior provides is:

B. The Truth *to Educate Us for Heaven*

No man ever had an audience with an earthly king without being carefully informed as to what was expected of him. How then can a sinner of Adam's race ever hope to stand before the King of the universe without the truth? Jesus said, "I am the truth." Get to know him before it is too late. Remember that heaven is a prepared place for a prepared people.

The third essential that our Savior provides is:

C. The Life *to Equip Us for Heaven*

Jesus declared, "Unless one is born again, he cannot see the kingdom of God" (John 3:3). How can a man who has lived without God on earth be introduced suddenly into a realm of perfect life and holiness? Would he care for it? Could he live in it? The answer is no. He could no more live in heaven than a fish, taken from the depths of the sea, could live in the pure light and beauty of the sunshine. It would be out of its element and the environment would be contrary to every instinct of its nature. The same is true of you and me. In our fallen nature, we could not subsist in the realms of glory without "life from above" experienced *now!* No wonder Jesus insists, "I am the life." Paul, writing of the mystery of the gospel which takes sinners to heaven, urges that the guarantee of reaching the Father's house is, "Christ in you, the hope of glory" (Col. 1:27).

Conclusion

Can you say that Christ is in you? O, may the certainty, the concept, the completeness, the community, and the commendation of heaven lead you to say:

> To Christ the Way, the Truth, the Life,
> I come, no more to roam;
> He'll guide me to my "Father's house,"
> To my eternal home.
>
> James McGranahan

10

Is There a Hell to Shun?

Luke 16:19–31

> There was a certain rich man. . . . The rich man also died
> and was buried. And being in torments in Hades, . . . he
> cried and said, "Father Abraham, have mercy on me." . . .
> But Abraham said, ". . . between us and you there is a great
> gulf fixed, so that those who want to pass from here to you
> cannot, nor can those from there pass to us."
>
> Luke 16:19–26

Introduction

There is no more solemn story in the whole of the Bible
than the one in our text. It appears that it was occasioned
by the very foolish attitude adopted by the Pharisees to the
Savior's sermon on worldliness and materialism. Christ had
been warning against the folly of serving mammon while
forgetting God. And we read that the covetous Pharisees
who heard these things "derided Him" (Luke 16:14). So the
Lord Jesus drew aside the curtain of man's future destiny
to show His hearers how life in eternity is determined by

life in time. And the latter end of two men is revealed. The one, who lived for God even in spite of adverse circumstances, is carried to heaven's happiness. The other, who lived for self in spite of all His privileges and opportunities, is found tormented in hell.

This story is designed to sum up the Lord's teaching on the subject of hell. No one ever spoke more plainly, frequently, and solemnly on hell than the Savior. But as is usual with men, there was a tendency among His hearers merely to treat His teaching as objective doctrine and nothing more. So the Lord tells this story to show how relevant and personal is the question of a hell to shun. Will you follow as I seek to retell it and discover some of the solemn emphases? First of all, observe how this story teaches:

I. The Fact of Hell

"A certain rich man . . . died and was buried . . . in Hades . . . he cried" (Luke 16:19, 22–24). With these awful words, the Savior confronts us with the inescapable fact of hell. If it is true that symbolical language is used, let us not imagine that this in any way weakens the gravity of the situation. Remember that none other than the Son of God chose the symbolism. Remember, moreover, that figurative expression was chosen to convey a true impression. If you think that the symbolism is terrible, then the words have fulfilled their purpose; for the truth behind them is more terrible still. Bearing this in mind, notice then that hell has to do with:

A. The Fact of a Person

"There was a certain rich man," a person whose indifference, indulgence, and infidelity led him to die without God and without hope. Then he reappears in hell with a capacity to see, hear, speak, feel, and remember.

Whether this certain man was a real or fictitious person in the story makes no difference. Because the rich

man had a specific number of brothers (five) and because
the poor man was given a proper name (Lazarus), it is
likely that this is a true story. Be that as it may, the point
Jesus was driving home was that hell is personal. Fur-
thermore, we should keep steadily before our minds the
possible damnation, not of our enemies nor of our friends
(since both of these disturb the reason), but of ourselves.
The story is not about your wife or your son, nor about
Judas Iscariot or Hitler; it is about you and me.

Moreover, hell has to do with:

B. The Fact of a Place

"In Hades . . . he cried." Whether this is a location or
a condition or both is not the central issue. We know that
Jesus spoke of hell as a place to establish the fact. It is an
unseen realm, for that is the meaning of the word *hades,*
which is here translated hell. It is a state that is associated with suffering, because the rich man in the story calls
it "this place of torment" (Luke 16:28). It is a sphere into
which souls pass after death. What is more important and
manifestly clear, however, is that hell is a fact—a fact not
only in Scripture, but a fact in our own minds.

We all know of heavens and hells on earth. We have
all come across men in whose heart the fire of remorse
and the worm of accusing conscience have created a ver-
itable hell. But there is something in our own mind that
tells us that such earthly hells are but a foretaste of what
awaits the man who, spurning the mercy of God, dies red-
handed in sinful rebellion. This is why Robert Browning
wrote, "There may be heaven, there must be hell."

C. S. Lewis, writing on hell, says, "There is no doctrine
that I would more willingly remove from Christianity
than this, if it lay in my power. But it has the full support of Scripture, and specially of our Lord's own words;
it has always been held by Christendom, and has the
support of reason." Later he adds, "I said glibly a moment
ago that I would pay 'any price' to remove this *doctrine.*

I lied. I could not pay one fractional part of the price that
God has already paid to remove the *fact.*"[1]

Returning to our text again, I want you to consider in the
second place:

II. The Flame of Hell

"I am tormented in this flame" (Luke 16:24). These are ter-
rifying words but are nonetheless truthful! They reveal the
horrors that await the men and women who choose to go to
hell. The action of the flame of torment on the human personality must be unimaginably dreadful. From our Lord's
own words, we would judge that the torments of hell result
from:

A. The Flame of an Uncleansed Conscience

"Son, remember that in your lifetime you received
your good things" (Luke 16:25). This man, in common
with all who go to hell, was guilty of spiritual sins. He
had received all the "good things" of life without a thought
for God. As a son of Abraham, he knew, as any intelligent man knows, that, "Every good gift and every perfect gift is from above, and comes down from the Father
of lights, with whom there is no variation or shadow of
turning" (James 1:17). But even with this knowledge, he
chose to leave God out of his reckoning and therefore
out of his life. In other words, he deliberately and defi-
antly committed the spiritual sin that damns men's souls.
For "to him who knows to do good and does not do it,
to him it is sin" (James 4:17).

During his lifetime, he was able to escape the intense
heat of the flame of an uncleansed conscience. But now
it was, "Son, remember." O the pangs of guilt, regret, and
remorse of an uncleansed conscience!

The torments of hell also result from:

B. The Flame of an Unsatisfied Capacity

"Then he cried and said, 'Father Abraham, have mercy on me, and send Lazarus that he may dip the tip of his finger in water and cool my tongue'" (Luke 16:24). Only those who have been deprived of that which satisfies a created and developed capacity can appreciate something of the hellish torments of this flame. This man, also in common with all who go to hell, was guilty of selfish sins. He had lived for self-gratification. He had therefore created and developed a capacity that nothing but his selfish tongue could satisfy. But now there was not even the representative drop of water to satisfy the craving void of an unsatisfied capacity. Well has someone said that the law of habit makes a man's hell.

The torments of hell further result from:

C. The Flame of an Unrelieved Concern

"I have five brothers" (Luke 16:28). This man, again in common with all who go to hell, was guilty of social sins. Whether his five brothers were blood relations or representative of the people he influenced during his lifetime makes no difference. The point is that he never cared for them until he passed into hell. But now the flame of unfulfilled social obligations exposes his sins. He realizes the truth of the saying, "None of us lives to himself, and no one dies to himself" (Rom. 14:7).

Illustration

A student, enrolled in a seminary course on preaching, submitted a sermon outline titled "Things in Hell That Belong in Church." At first the professor was skeptical about the contents of an outline with such a sensational title. On further examination, he was satisfied that the sermon made some very good observations. After several points on things like genuine faith in God, and heartfelt sorrow for sin, there was a point based on Jesus' story of the rich man and Lazarus (Luke 16:19–31). Referring to the rich man's

request for a special evangelist for his five surviving brothers, the student emphasized that one thing in hell that
belongs in church is a burden for the lost![2]

God demands first, love for himself; second, love for
our neighbors; and then love for ourselves. But this man
had changed the divine order and was now paying the
price. If he were not concerned with the salvation of men
during his lifetime, he was certainly concerned now,
and, sadly, would be eternally unrelieved of that concern, for the inferences of Scripture suggest that the retri-
bution for social sins is eternal loneliness.

So we have been permitted a glimpse into the eternal
hell of torment. God is never said to torture or torment
souls in hell. We should never think of accusing the
monarch or president of any country of torturing his subjects who, by reason of their misdeeds, find themselves
the inmates of the nation's prisons! As on earth, so in
hell, the prisoners themselves determined their own torment. Well did David write long, long ago, "The wicked
is snared in the work of his own hands" (Ps. 9:16).

For the honor of the Word and to the glory of God, it
is good to point out here, however, that the Bible ex-
pressly teaches degrees of punishment. There are to be
"few stripes" and "many stripes" (Luke 12:47–48). It is
to be "more tolerable" for some than for others (Matt.
11:20–24). For everyone there will be the most exact
weighing of privilege, knowledge, and opportunity. Righteous judgment will be meted out.

A careful study of the story before us teaches yet another
truth:

III. The Finality of Hell

"Now . . . you are tormented," said Abraham. "And
besides all this, between us and you there is a great gulf

fixed" (Luke 16:25–26). While this story primarily concerns Hades and not Gehenna, which is the final abode of the lost, it clearly and solemnly teaches the finality of hell. In other words:

A. The Finality of Hell's Sentence

"Now . . . you are tormented" (16:25). That this sentence is final is clearly indicated and corroborated by the rest of Scripture. Examine, for example, our Lord's solemn warnings about hell and you will find that in every instance the sentence is always expressed in words that denote finality. Think for a moment of the three main symbols that Jesus used in His declaration on this subject:

1. PUNISHMENT

"And these will go away into everlasting punishment" (Matt. 25:46). There is nothing revocable about that sentence. It is final.

Illustration

A profane man, who was being taken down into a coal mine by a Christian miner, said as they descended the depth and the air grew hotter and hotter, "It's terribly hot; I wonder how far it is to hell?"

The Christian solemnly replied, "I cannot tell you the distance in terms of meters or miles, but if one link of that chain were to give way, you might be there in a minute and you would be separated forever."

2. DESTRUCTION

Speaking about the fear of God as against the fear of man and devils, Jesus said, "Fear Him who is able to destroy both soul and body in hell" (Matt. 10:28). By *destruction* the Savior could never have meant annihilation, for the annihilation of the soul is intrinsically impossible. Moreover, the torment of hell presupposes a condition that requires a living entity; and you cannot torment what is annihilated. Like the punishment, therefore, the destruction must be eternal. Paul supports this when he tells us,

> When the Lord Jesus is revealed from heaven with His mighty angels, in flaming fire taking vengeance on those who do not know God, and on those who do not obey the gospel of our Lord Jesus Christ. These shall be punished with everlasting destruction from the presence of the Lord and from the glory of His power.
>
> 2 Thessalonians 1:7–9

3. BANISHMENT

Referring to religious people who would not bend to His authority, Jesus said that they "will be cast out into outer darkness. There will be weeping and gnashing of teeth" (Matt. 8:12). Half measures are impossible in view of the cross. The day is passed when God could plead with men about their sins. The controversy now is not about a broken law, but a rejected Christ.

The sentence is final. There is no suggestion of a second chance in the Bible. And this is no reflection on the love of God. I believe that if a million chances would do any good, they would be given. The end must come sometime, and it does not require a very robust faith to believe that Omniscience knows when. "Shall not the Judge of all the earth do right?" (Gen. 18:25).

B. The Finality of Hell's Separation

"There is a great gulf fixed." Hell fixes and finalizes all that separates a soul from God. Man's heart will not be altered by a reversal of circumstances. Men who hate the gospel now will hate it then. Punishment has never changed the man who has fixed his choice. Did punishment ever gain the heart of Cain? Did heavy judgments ever soften Pharaoh's will or change his attitude toward God? Was Ahab ever moved to repentance by what overtook him? Did the demons, who spoke to Christ and prayed, ever once cry for mercy?

And what do we learn, in this regard, from the story before us? You will notice by a careful reading that the rich man in hell did not request salvation for himself. There seemed to be no desire whatsoever for spiritual grace. No doubt this condition interprets those fearful words that describe the fixation point of all the damned, "He who is unjust, let him be unjust still; he who is filthy, let him be filthy still" (Rev. 22:11). Someone has written, "As the tree falls, so shall it lie."

There is a hell to shun! The fact is indisputable, the flame is inescapable, and the finality is irrevocable. To those of you who might be tempted by a heartless devil to object to this solemn doctrine, let me put the following questions: What are you asking God to do? To wipe out your past sins and give you a new start? He has done this at Calvary. To forgive you? You will not be forgiven unless you receive Him. To leave you alone? Alas, I am afraid that is what He will have to do, and unless you repent, hell is inevitable.

Is it any wonder that God, in love, has punctuated his revelation at every conceivable point with such warnings as, "It is appointed for men to die once, but after this the judgment" (Heb. 9:27). "He has appointed a day on which He will judge the world" (Acts 17:31). "Because there is wrath, beware lest He take you away with one blow; for a large ransom would not help you avoid it" (Job 36:18). "Knowing, therefore, the terror of the Lord, we persuade men" (2 Cor. 5:11).

When the rich man in hell pleaded that his five brothers be spared the torments of a lost eternity, Abraham answered, "They have Moses and the prophets; let them hear them" (Luke 16:29). The imprisoned man pleaded further, "If one goes to them from the dead, they will repent" (v. 30). But Abraham replied, "If they do not hear Moses and the prophets, neither will they be persuaded though one rise from the dead" (v. 31). My friend, if ever you find yourself in hell (God forbid it!), it will be because you have:

1. Ridiculed the Writings of Moses

Jesus says, "If you believed Moses, you would believe Me; for he wrote about Me. But if you do not believe his writings, how will you believe My words?" (John 5:46–47).

2. Refused the Witness of the Prophets

Remember that it is recorded, "To Him [the Lord Jesus] all the prophets witness that, through His name, whoever believes in Him will receive remission of sins" (Acts 10:43).

3. Rejected the Warnings of Christ

"Most assuredly, I say to you, he who hears My word and believes in Him who sent Me has everlasting life, and shall not come into judgment, but has passed from death into life" (John 5:24).

Whether from Moses, the prophets, or Jesus Himself, the message is one: A Christless life means a Christless eternity, and a Christless eternity *is* hell.

Conclusion

What will you do then with Jesus who is called Christ? Will you accept Him and gain heaven? Or will you reject Him and earn hell?

11

The Confession of Sin

Proverbs 28:11–14

> He who covers his sins will not prosper, but whoever confesses and forsakes them will have mercy.
>
> Proverbs 28:13

Introduction

God made man to walk in light. That is why Christians are called "children of light" (Eph. 5:8). Adam and Eve were clothed with light until they sinned. At that moment fear, nakedness, shame, darkness, and death followed in swift succession.

And this is the way it has been since that first tragic fall in the Garden of Eden. The theme of the Bible from that point onward is man's restoration to fellowship with God. Our Heavenly Father loves the creatures of his hand and longs to fellowship with them in light. This is why John writes,

> This is the message which we have heard of Him and declare to you, that God is light and in Him is no darkness at all. If we say that we have fellowship with Him, and walk in dark-

ness, we lie and do not practice the truth. But if we walk in the light as He is in the light, we have fellowship with one another, and the blood of Jesus Christ His Son cleanses us from all sin. If we say that we have no sin, we deceive ourselves, and the truth is not in us. If we confess our sins, He is faithful and just to forgive us our sins and to cleanse us from all unrighteousness. If we say that we have not sinned, we make Him a liar, and His word is not in us.

1 John 1:5–10

With such a statement of truth before us, we can understand what is meant by the confession of sin. Solomon puts it succinctly when he says, "He who covers his sins will not prosper, but whoever confesses and forsakes them will have mercy." This confession of sin teaches us three things:

I. The Folly of Deceitfulness

"He who covers his sins will not prosper" (Prov. 28:13). The Bible reminds us that "the heart [of man] is deceitful above all things, and desperately wicked" (Jer. 17:9), and further states, "If we say that we have no sin, we deceive ourselves, and the truth is not in us" (1 John 1:8). Inherent in every one of us is the propensity not only to sin, but also to cover it up. So we have:

A. The Practice of Deceitfulness

"He who covers his sins will not prosper." There are various as well as devious ways in which sinners and saints alike conceal their wrongdoing. Some try to cover sin by excusing it, like Ananias and Sapphira. You will remember that they gave only part of their gift to God instead of the whole and imagined that such lying would be excused. Peter said, "Why has Satan filled your heart to lie to the Holy Spirit and keep back part of the price of the land for yourself . . . You have not lied to men but to God" (Acts 5:3–4). And judgment swiftly followed.

Some cover up by exploiting sin, like the antinomianists of Paul's day. He had to address them in stern words when he asked, "Shall we continue in sin that grace may abound?" (Rom. 6:1). Believe it or not, there are people like this today. They imagine that they can turn the grace of God into licentiousness (Jude 4). The more they sin, the more they think they can sing, "Amazing grace! How sweet the sound, that saved a wretch like me!" But Paul retorts, Perish the thought! As we shall see later, God never forgives what isn't confessed or forsaken.

Some cover up by enjoying sin, for the Bible states that there are "the passing pleasures of sin" (Heb. 11:25). Eve took the fruit of the tree because she "saw that the tree was good for food, that it was pleasant to the eyes, and a tree desirable to make one wise" (Gen. 3:6). But in eating that fruit she not only involved Adam, her husband, in sin, but also cursed the human race. Gehazi, Elisha's servant, coveted the gifts that Naaman offered in gratitude for his cleansing from leprosy, but for those few moments of pleasure he became a leper for the rest of his life (2 Kings 5:20–27).

So I could go on illustrating. There are many ways in which people try to conceal sin in their lives, but all such deceitfulness is futile because "God requires an account of what is past" (Eccles. 3:15). And He reminds us that "there is nothing covered that will not be revealed, nor hidden that will not be known" (Luke 12:2).

With the practice of deceitfulness there is also:

B. The Peril of Deceitfulness

"He who covers his sins will not prosper." Whatever the outward appearances, the deceitful person is headed for serious trouble. For one thing, such a man or woman lives a lie, and there is nothing God hates more than hypocrisy. Read what Jesus had to say to the hypocrites of his day (Matthew 23). For another thing, such a life of deceitfulness precludes forgiveness. God pardons only the penitent, and such penitence is impossible without an admission of guilt. What is even worse, the practice of deceitfulness confirms the sinner in his sin. Covering up sin never destroys it. Indeed, it is no more killed than the seed of a poisoned plant, when sown in the soil. Sooner or later it will spring forth in an even greater harvest of evil. David knew something about this when he cried, "When I kept silent, my bones grew old through my groaning all the day long. For day and night Your hand was heavy upon me" (Ps. 32:3). He discovered that the longer he hid his sin, the more agony he endured. So we see what is meant by the folly of deceitfulness.

This confession of sin further teaches us:

II. The Duty of Disclosure

"He who covers his sins will not prosper, but whoever confesses and forsakes them will have mercy" (Prov. 28:13). The confessing and forsaking of sin are more than good therapy; they are divine requirements. We have only to read David's psalm of penitence (Psalm 51) to see this exemplified in practical experience. The fallen king spells out the need for openness and transparency when he says, "You desire truth in the inward parts, and in the hidden part You will make me to know wisdom" (Ps. 51:6). From our text we learn that this duty of disclosure is twofold:

A. Sin Must Be Admitted

"Whoever confesses [his sins]." The Bible teaches that confession of sin is personal, social, and general. It is personal when it has to do with one's own fellowship with God. Whenever sin interrupts that fellowship there should be no delay in confessing the known sin and seeking restored fellowship. The apostle John makes this clear when he affirms, "If we confess our sins, He is faithful and just to forgive us our sins and to cleanse us from all unrighteousness" (1 John 1:9).

Confession is personal. It involves three things. First, we should tell God about our sins. God intends that we should not only name them, but also *nail* them! Notice the word *sins* is in the plural. Nothing should be covered up. Then we should *trust* God about our sins. Because of the Word of God in Christ and the work of God in Christ, our heavenly Father is both "faithful and just to forgive us our sins and to cleanse us from all unrighteousness." And third, we are to *thank* God for forgiving our sins. Until we can look up into his face and say thank you, we have not trusted Him, and that is usually because we have not told Him about our sins. Only when we say thank you, will we know the smile of His favor and the joy of His forgiveness.

Confession is also social. The Bible says, "Confess your trespasses to one another, and pray for one another, that you may be healed" (James 5:16). And Jesus taught, "If you bring your gift to the altar, and there remember that your brother has something against you, leave your gift there before the altar, and go your way. First be reconciled to your brother, and then come and offer your gift" (Matt. 5:23–24). This aspect of confession is what is often lacking in local assemblies today. Until we put relationships right between one another we can never expect God to hear us or bless us. Jesus taught this explicitly when He declared, "If you forgive men their trespasses, your heavenly Father will also forgive you. But if you do not forgive men their trespasses, neither will your Father forgive your trespasses" (Matt. 6:14–15).

Then there is such a thing as general confession. This is when wrongdoing affects the whole church. You will remember that the people confessed their sins before John the Baptist (Matt. 3:6) and before the apostles (Acts 19:18). Among the Jews, the high priest acted as the mouthpiece of the people on the great Day of Atonement by confessing their iniquities publicly and laying them on the scapegoat. But more than this, every trespass offering was a public recognition of guilt. This is why the offender had to come forward and lay his hand on the head of the victim (Lev. 1:4). This is what discipline in the local church is all about. Would to God that we returned to these divine principles before judgment falls on the religious life of our day!

B. Sin Must Be Abandoned

"Whoever confesses and forsakes [his sins] will have mercy." True confession must be accompanied by repentance. Without such renunciation of sin, our approach to God for forgiveness and cleansing is nothing more than mockery. Forsaking sin involves action. Such action calls for an apology. Sometimes it calls for reconciliation with a brother or sister. And it may call for restitution.

Illustration

F. E. Marsh tells of an occasion when he preached on the subject of restitution. After the service a man came to him and said, "Pastor, you have put me in a bad fix. I've stolen from my employer and am ashamed to tell him about it. You see, I'm a boatbuilder, and the man I work for is an unbeliever. I have often talked to him about Christ, but he only laughs at me. In my work, expensive copper nails are used because they won't rust in water. I've been taking some of them home for a boat I am building in my backyard. I'm afraid if I tell my boss what I've done and offer to pay for them, he'll think I'm a hypocrite, and I'll never be able to reach him for Christ. Yet my conscience is bothered."

Later when the man saw the preacher again he exclaimed, "Pastor, I've settled the matter and I'm so relieved." The minister asked, "What happened when you told your boss?" "Oh, he looked at me intently and said, 'George, I've always thought you were a hypocrite, but now I'm not so sure. Maybe there's something in your Christianity after all. Any religion that makes a man admit he's been stealing a few copper nails and offer to settle for them must be worth having.'"[1]

That story helps to point out what we mean by confessing and forsaking sin.

This brings us to another aspect of the confession of sin:

III. The Glory of Deliverance

"Whoever confesses and forsakes [his sins] will have mercy" (Prov. 28:13). The mercy of God is one of the great themes of biblical revelation. Indeed, David tells us that God's mercy "reaches unto the heavens" (Ps. 57:10). He talks about "the multitude of [God's] mercy" (Ps. 69:13). He sings about a God "abundant in mercy" (Ps. 86:15). He exults in the mercy of the Lord that "endures forever" (Ps. 106:1). It is in that mercy that we find the glory of deliverance for men and women who are prepared to confess and forsake their sins. Notice that this glorious deliverance comes through God's great mercy.

A. The Mercy of the Father's Pardon

"Whoever confesses and forsakes [his sins] will have mercy." Isaiah the prophet helps us to understand something of the Father's pardon when he writes, "Let the wicked forsake his way, and the unrighteous man his thoughts; let him return unto the LORD, and He will have mercy on him; and to our God, for He will abundantly pardon" (Isa. 55:7). We have already cited the New Testament equivalent of this verse where John declares, "If we confess our sins, He [God the Father] is faithful and just to forgive us our sins and to cleanse us from all unrighteousness" (1 John 1:9). Because of the atoning sacrifice of the Lord Jesus Christ, God can have mercy on us and "abundantly pardon" all who are prepared to confess and forsake their sins. How wonderful to know that there is a glorious way of deliverance from sin and its guilt and that we can be *clean* before a holy God!

Illustration

A little boy was trying to explain what we do when we attend church. He understood the matter but he had trouble with the pronunciation. He meant to say, "We go to church to worship." What he said was, "We go to church to *wash up!*"[2]

Indeed we do! We go to find the cleansing of God's grace. We go for reassurance of His love. We go to hear again the news that never gets old and is always good news: Christ came into the world to save sinners.

B. The Mercy of the Savior's Presence

"Whoever confesses and forsakes [his sins] will have mercy." There is a sense in which the Lord Jesus never leaves us or forsakes us, however seriously we sin. On the other hand, it is right to say that the realization of His presence is lost when we walk in darkness. This is what the apostle John means when he writes, "If we say that we have fellowship with Him, and walk in darkness, we lie and do not practice the truth. But if we walk in the light as He is in the light, we have fellowship with one another, and the blood of Jesus Christ His Son cleanses us from all sin" (1 John 1:6–7). The secret of knowing the presence of the Lord Jesus, moment by moment, is having a relationship with Him that is untainted by sin, with the ungrieved, unquenched Holy Spirit filling our hearts. This is what walking in the light is all about.

It is comforting to know that we have a high priest who is touched with every feeling of our infirmities because He was tempted in all points just as we are, yet without sin. Because of this we can "come boldly to the throne of grace, that we may obtain *mercy* and find grace to help in the time of need" (Heb. 4:16, italics mine). This is the mercy of the Savior's presence.

C. The Mercy of the Spirit's Power

"Whoever confesses and forsakes [his sins] will have mercy." Paul reminds us that "according to His mercy He saved us, through the washing of regeneration and renewing of the Holy Spirit, whom He poured out on us abundantly through Jesus Christ our Savior" (Titus 3:5–6). The Living Bible paraphrases this, "He saved us—not because we were good enough to be saved, but because of his kindness [or mercy] . . . by washing away our sins and giving us the new joy of the indwelling Holy Spirit whom he poured out upon us with wonderful fullness—and all because of what Jesus Christ our Savior did."

We can all remember that initial joy that came into our souls when the Holy Spirit regenerated us. But the greater thing about the Christian life is that the power of the Holy Spirit becomes even more evident in our lives as we "grow in the grace and knowledge of our Lord and Savior Jesus Christ" (2 Peter 3:18). This power enables us to live and to serve to the glory of God.

We all know, however, that when we sin, God's power in our lives is nullified. This happened again and again to the early disciples, and they had to confess their sins and seek a new fullness and anointing of the Spirit. This is why the apostle Paul exhorts the Ephesian believers to "have no fellowship with the unfruitful works of darkness" and then adds, "And do not be drunk with wine, in which is dissipation; but be filled with the Spirit" (Eph. 5:11, 18). Only when we "walk in the light" can we be filled with the Spirit, and only when we are filled with the Spirit can we know His power in our lives.

Conclusion

This is the glorious deliverance that God affords to those who are prepared to confess their sins. It is nothing less than the mercy of the Father's pardon, the mercy of the Savior's presence, and the mercy of the Spirit's power.

What lessons we have learned as we have worked our way through this remarkable text! Remember what I said at the beginning: God created man to walk in light. Let us see to it that we confess our sins as we tread "the path of the just [which] is like the shining sun, that shines ever brighter unto the perfect day" (Prov. 4:18).

12

God's New Creation

2 Corinthians 5:16–21

If anyone is in Christ, he is a new creation; old things have passed away; behold, all things have become new.

2 Corinthians 5:17

Introduction

The Lord Jesus summed up the great purpose of His coming to earth, when He said, "I have come that they may have life, and that they may have it more abundantly" (John 10:10). What a breathtaking truth!—life more abundant. Do you know what that means in your experience? This abundant life is God's new creation. In the light of our text, I want you to notice:

I. The Sphere of This New Creation

"If anyone is *in Christ*" (2 Cor. 5:17, italics mine). There are at least five spheres or realms in which God's creative power is demonstrated, namely, the mineral, vegetable, animal, human, and spiritual realms.

A. *Mineral*

The mineral realm cannot force its way up into the vegetable kingdom. It is a sphere of its own, where God's creative power is made known in the handiwork of geology.

B. *Vegetable*

The vegetable realm has the power to reach down and incorporate into its texture the rich metals of the mineral sphere but it cannot force its way up into the animal kingdom. Here again, it is a realm of its own, where God's creative power is revealed in the beauties of botany.

C. *Animal*

The animal realm has power to reach down to the vegetable sphere and feed its life on the food of that kingdom, but it cannot force its way up into the human. There are at least twelve bridges on four levels that the evolutionist must cross before he can relate animal creation to human creation. These levels may be set forth as follows:

1. Physical Level

With its bridges of form, chromosome count, and substance.

2. Mental Level

With its bridges of speech, invention, and mathematics.

3. MORAL LEVEL

With its bridges of conscience, influence, and character.

4. SPIRITUAL LEVEL

With its bridges of sin, regeneration, and immortality.

So we see that the animal sphere is a realm of its own, where the great Creator displays His wisdom in zoology.

D. Human

The human has power to reach down to the animal sphere and cultivate an intimacy with the most intelligent of the creatures of that kingdom, but he cannot force his way up into the spiritual realm. This is why Jesus said to an educated religious leader, "Unless one is born again, he cannot see the kingdom of God" (John 3:3). And again, "That which is born of the flesh is flesh, and that which is born of the Spirit is spirit" (v. 6).

So once again we see that the human sphere is a realm of its own, where God manifests the wonders of anthropology. Thus the psalmist sings, "I will praise You, for I am fearfully and wonderfully made" (Ps. 139:14).

E. Spiritual

The spiritual has power to appreciate and in a measure, control all other spheres. Before the fall, it is recorded, Adam enjoyed such spiritual ascendancy. The psalmist declares, "You have made him to have dominion over the works of Your hands; You have put all things under his feet" (Ps. 8:6).

So we see that the spiritual man is God's highest creation. The sphere of this creation is defined in our text as "in Christ." In another place Paul reminds us that, "We are His workmanship, created in Christ Jesus" (Eph. 2:10). Before a man can be spiritual, however, he must be born into a new realm or sphere. The character of the sphere cannot be changed to suit the sinful nature of man. So man himself must be changed if he would dwell in the kingdom of God. The manner in which God changes a man not only constitutes the message of the gospel, but displays the glories of His love. This leads us to consider:

II. The Scope of This New Creation

"If anyone is in Christ, he is a new creation; old things have passed away; behold, all things have become new" (2 Cor. 5:17). The scope of this new creation is magnificently summed up in these words, "Old things have passed away; . . . all things have become new." God says to us, "Put on the new man which was created according to God, in righteousness and true holiness" (Eph. 4:24). What an offer this is! God's own life of victorious righteousness and spotless holiness is made available for people like you and me. But the truth goes even deeper, when we learn that:

A. God Crucifies the Old

"Our old man was crucified with Him, that the body of sin might be done away with, that we should no longer be slaves of sin" (Rom. 6:6). In God's view the old creation, that sinful Adamic nature, was nailed to the cross when the Lord Jesus was crucified. To believe that truth is to be set free from the dominion of sin. The essence of this wonderful truth informs us that not only does God crucify the old, but wonder of wonders He creates the new!

B. God Creates the New

"For in Christ Jesus neither circumcision nor uncircumcision avails anything, but a new creation" (Gal. 6:15). There was a time when Paul judged men by human attainments. He praised those who best conformed to what he considered to be the demands of the Law. Then came the transforming experience, when God revealed to him that man could never be improved or patched up. He is rotten through and through. Nothing but a new creation avails. And so he asserts, "Therefore, from now on, we regard no one according to the flesh. Even though we have known Christ according to the flesh, yet now we know Him thus no longer. Therefore if anyone is in Christ, he is a new creation" (2 Cor. 5:16–17). Paul declares this, even though Christ must not be judged by His human attainments, but rather accepted as the *new creation* into which God wants to bring us. This, undoubtedly, is the thought the apostle has in mind when he affirms, "For as many of you as were baptized into Christ have put on Christ" (Gal. 3:27). So we have seen that it is a new creation that God offers. Old things are truly gone, and new things have come.

Illustration

It is a well-known fact that a caterpillar turns into a butterfly. There is certainly very little resemblance between the two, yet every butterfly has been a caterpillar. The butterfly can truly say, as he looks at the caterpillar, "Such was I, but now I am changed." So every Christian can look back to the time when he was a sinner and recognize that God has wrought a miraculous transformation.

The question now arises, "How may we know this new creation of God?" The answer to that question is our next point:

III. The Secret of This New Creation

"If anyone is in Christ, he is a new creation" (2 Cor. 5:17). And again, "All things are of God, who has reconciled us to Himself through Jesus Christ" (v. 18). In these two statements, we have the secret of this new creation of God—God's part and man's part. First, we have:

A. God's Welcome

"All things are of God, who has reconciled us to Himself through Jesus Christ." God welcomes us into this new life, with arms and hands that are bleeding and outstretched on a cross. For when the Son of God hung on that Roman gibbet, being made sin for us, "God was in Christ reconciling the world to Himself" (v. 19), that we might be made the righteousness of God in Him. Through the mystery of the cross, a new creation has been made available for you and me.

Illustration

A tough looking man was preaching in the open air. He was a saved drunkard who had formerly been a terror to himself, his family, and his neighbors. He was telling in all humility what great things God had done for him. A skeptic in the crowd began muttering and interjecting his infidel scoffs and jeers. "It's all a fancy and a dream," he sneered. A girl of ten years of age timidly touched the scoffer and whispered, "Please, sir, if it is a dream don't wake him— that's my daddy!" That touched the skeptic's heart and conscience. He was later converted and found that it was not a dream, but a *new creation!*

The other aspect of the secret is:

B. Man's Willingness

"If anyone is in Christ"; the conditional word *if* implies man's power to say yes or no. The door into the new life stands open for all, but the man who enters it must demonstrate true willingness. Will you enter now?

Illustration

The sphere, scope, and secret of this new creation are beautifully illustrated by the familiar Old Testament story of Noah and the ark. You will remember how God had passed righteous judgment on the sin, corruption, and uselessness of the old creation; and at the same time He warned Noah that the only hope of a new creation and a new beginning was to be found in the ark. You will recall how Noah entered

the ark and found it even as God had said, for in due time
he emerged into a new beginning.

Conclusion

My friend, Christ is that ark. He is God's provision for you.
The open door is God's welcome into a new creation. Will
you enter *now?* "If anyone is in Christ, he is a new creation."

13

Life with a Minus

Mark 10:17–25

One came running, knelt before Him, and asked Him, "Good Teacher, what shall I do that I may inherit eternal life?" . . . Then Jesus, looking at him, loved him, and said to him, "One thing you lack: Go your way, sell whatever you have and give to the poor, and you will have treasure in heaven; and come, take up the cross, and follow Me." But he was sad at this word, and went away grieved, for he had great possessions.

Mark 10:17, 21–22

Introduction

When we read the Bible and observe human life, it seems that for a lot of people the failure to be *truly* Christian is not so much that they are utterly degraded, as that they are "minus that spiritual plus," that extra something that makes a lovely and charming personality the best that God has purposed for mankind.

Look at the remarkable story of the young ruler, as told by the Gospel writers. Here we have aspiration, personality, and charm, but with all this, it is life with a minus. First, let us consider how life with a minus expressed itself:

I. The Young Man's Longing

"Good Teacher," he asked, "what shall I do that I may inherit eternal life?" (Mark 10:17). There we have his longing, his quest, the call of his unsatisfied heart. This quest for eternal life is far more widespread than we sometimes imagine. Indeed, the fact is that this longing is inherent in man's very nature. The Bible says that God "has put 'eternity' in their hearts" (Eccles. 3:11). In other words, God has put a hunger in our life that no one but He can satisfy. Someone has said, "Man has a vast capacity for God, and a vast emptiness without Him." And this is true of all people. The longing may find a thousand means of expression, some of them entirely unworthy, but it is there. When it rises to its noblest form of expression, it employs the very words of this young man, "What shall I do that I may inherit eternal life?" This young man meant business. Observe his haste, his humility, and his hunger:

A. His Haste

"One came running" (Mark 10:17). He regarded the matter as urgent, as well as important.

B. His Humility

He "knelt" (Mark 10:17). In spite of the fact that Jesus wore the garb of the peasant, and the inquirer in all probability wore the purple of wealth and was a ruler among his people, he was humble enough to kneel.

Illustration

While Mark does not identify the man, Luke calls him a "ruler" (18:18) meaning that he was probably a member of an official council. Matthew (19:20) tells us that he was "young." All this to say that kneeling before Jesus was a highly significant act.

Stephen Olford relates: During my many years in Africa, kneeling to ask a favor was a sign of respect and earnest desire, especially among a tribe known as the Achokive who claimed that "they would kneel to no one!"

C. His Hunger

He "asked" (Mark 10:17). In Jesus he recognized the source of eternal life and the answer to his hungry soul. There was a minus in his life, a deep longing; hence this approach to Christ.

Have you a longing for a higher quality of life? You know you have! Do not hesitate in coming to Christ now.

Second, the Savior described the minus as:

II. The Young Man's Lack

Jesus said to him, "One thing you lack" (Mark 10:21). If you look at this fine fellow, you will agree with me that he has everything for which one could wish. But the Savior insisted that he was lacking one thing. What was it?

A. Was It a Physical Lack?

From the story given us here, I think not. He was young; that is clearly stated. He was fit; that can be inferred from his running. He was attractive and charming; that is surely implied by our Lord's reactions. Indeed, it is recorded that, "Jesus, looking at him, loved him" (Mark 10:21); that is, Jesus loved his manhood.

B. Was It a Material Lack?

Here again the answer is no, for we read that "he had great possessions" (Mark 10:22).

C. Was It a Social Lack?

No. Luke tells us that he was a "ruler" (Luke 18:18) of his people, and that at an early age. From all accounts, it would seem that he was a most popular young man.

D. Was It a Moral Lack?

Once again, the answer is no, for when Jesus measured him up against the second table of the Law, the young man replied, "All these I have observed from my youth" (Mark 10:19–20). In other words, My conduct before men has always been characterized by the strictest morality. And this was no empty boast, for we notice that the Lord did not attempt to contradict him.

E. The Lacking Relationship

And yet there was one thing lacking, without which life for this young man was an eternal minus. If the life of this young man fell short of God's standard, what about your life? Strange as it may seem, his lack is your lack, because in the final analysis, God does not judge men from the human standpoint. In fact this is our clue to the minus in this young man's life. He said he kept the *second* table of the Law, that is, his relationship to man. But what about the *first* table of the Law, the four commandments that Jesus did not quote? The silence of Jesus on the first four commandments was intended to bring home to this young man his lack: *his relationship to God,* the vital minus. God was missing in his life, and this explains his lack of satisfaction and harmony. Perhaps this explains why *your* life is without satisfaction and harmony.

Illustration

With great relish, G. Campbell Morgan, the great London preacher, used to recall an occasion when he visited Denver, Colorado, to conduct a series of meetings. His train was late and he was hurried from it to the church, where the congregation was waiting. He went onto the platform in the company of the minister. As the hymn was announced, his eyes caught sight of the pipes of a magnificent organ. But when the hymn was introduced, he heard the wheezy notes of a little reed organ beneath the elevated platform. He turned to his friend, the minister, and asked, "What is the matter with the great organ?" The pastor replied, "There is nothing the matter with it. It cost fifty thousand dollars." But Dr. Morgan retorted, "Well, why is it not being played?" "I'm sorry, it lacks one thing," explained the minister with a twinkle in his eye. "What is that?" "Why," said the minister, "a musician!"

Do you see the purpose of the illustration? The church possessed a magnificent instrument made to catch the wind and transmute it into music, but not a sound, not a note, for the lack of an organist! That is *you,* my friend. Your human life is God-created, an instrument designed to catch the music of heaven and express it on earth, but you are silent. There is no music, no harmony, no satisfaction *in* your life or *from* your life.

The organ is also a picture of the rich young ruler. He lacked the Master-hand in his life. At this point, the rich young man could have found the spiritual plus, but in refusing to do what was needed, we read of:

III. The Young Man's Loss

"He ... went away grieved" (Mark 10:22). The young fellow balanced up the possibility of eternal life with the loss of his own soul; and for the temporary enjoyment of the lower, he refused the terms for the higher. His *longing* was his *lack,* and without Christ his lack was his loss.

We notice that as soon as Jesus revealed to him his vital lack, a relationship with God, He began to explain how that relationship to God could be established. In effect, He said that three factors were necessary:

A. A Christ-Centered Faith

"Go . . . sell . . . give . . . and come" (Mark 10:21), commanded the Savior. In those four words Jesus asked for a faith that was prepared to dethrone gold and enthrone God, a faith that would sacrifice any rival or substitute to the Lord Jesus.

This is the faith that Jesus wants from you: a faith that *will receive* and enthrone him in your heart—now! Without Christ reigning in your life, as Savior and Lord, you cannot be related to God. Make this your witness:

> The dearest idol I have known,
> Whate'er that idol be,
> Help me to tear it from Thy throne,
> And worship only Thee.
>
> William Cowper

The second necessary factor was:

B. A Christ-Conditioned Fellowship

"Take up the cross" (Mark 10:21), challenged the Savior. The Lord Jesus was calling for an all-out willingness to share the fellowship of suffering with Jesus (see Philippians 3:10). The apostle Paul considered no ambition more worthy of realization than that of sharing in the sufferings of Christ, in order to experience the glory of His risen life. He could say, "I also count all things loss . . . that I may know Him and the power of His resurrection, and the fellowship of His sufferings, being conformed to His death" (Phil. 3:8, 10).

Are you prepared to bow to the challenge of this Christ-conditioned fellowship? Then make this your prayer, "Lord Jesus, I take your cross of death to all of sin and self, that I may live your life of risen power."

The third necessary factor is:

C. A Christ-Controlled Following

"Follow Me" (Mark 10:21), commissioned the Savior. And a Christ-controlled following meant nothing less than hands, feet, eyes—all—given to the obedience of *Christ*, or "joining Christ in the *Way.*" (This is what *following* literally means.) Will you follow Christ like that and henceforth live only for Him? Then tell Him so without delay.

The Lord Jesus taught that relationship to God meant a Christ-centered faith, a Christ-conditioned fellowship, and a Christ-controlled following. In this relationship the Lord Jesus had purposed to:

1. SATISFY THIS YOUNG MAN'S LONGING

2. SUPPLY THIS YOUNG MAN'S LACK

3. SAVE THIS YOUNG MAN'S LOSS

But the young ruler turned away. Oh, the tragedy of it! May that never be said of you.

Illustration

The English portrait painter, George Frederick Watts, produced a masterpiece titled, "For He Had Great Possessions." It was a portrayal of the rich young ruler of our text. Looking at the painting, you will not see the young man's face. You will not even see a profile. You will see a three-quarter back view of the man. That back is turned on Jesus, and Watts has managed to paint in the droop of the shoulder and the flaccid hand, all the dejection of the man.

Like a ship passing in the moonlight, this young man had come for one brief moment into the gleam of the light on the water and then had slipped into darkness. And as far as we know, for that young ruler it was the darkness of a never-ending night.

He lacked the spiritual plus—a relationship to God. He could have found it in Christ but he refused to open his life to a Christ-centered faith, a Christ-conditioned fellowship, and a Christ-controlled following.

Conclusion

What about you? May it never be said that you turned away grieved.

Notes

Chapter 1: *The Grace of God*

1. Russell Lemon Jr. in a letter to his Bible school professor, February 28, 1989.

2. Walter Baxendale, *Dictionary of Illustrations for Pulpit and Platform* (Chicago: Moody, 1949), 224.

Chapter 3: *The Savior of Sinners*

1. Baxendale, *Dictionary of Illustrations,* 423, adapted.

2. Norman Grubb, *C. T. Studd: Cricketer and Pioneer* (London: Lutterworth Press, 1944), 141.

Chapter 5: *The Fate of Fruitlessness*

1. John Peter Lange, *Commentary on the Holy Scriptures,* vol. 8 (Grand Rapids: Zondervan, 1960), 380, adapted, used by permission.

2. Baxendale, *Dictionary of Illustrations,* 463, adapted.

3. A. Naismith, *1200 Notes, Quotes, and Anecdotes* (Chicago: Moody, 1962), 115.

Chapter 9: *Is There a Heaven to Gain?*

1. C. S. Lewis, *Mere Christianity* (New York: Macmillan, 1952), 119.

2. *Day by Day* with Billy Graham. ©1976 Billy Graham Evangelistic Association, used by permission, all rights reserved.

Chapter 10: *Is There a Hell to Shun?*

1. C. S. Lewis, *The Problem of Pain* (New York: Macmillan, 1962), 118–19.

2. From Robert F. Ramey at Grace Theological Seminary, Winona Lake, Ind., 1973.

Chapter 11: *The Confession of Sin*

1. F. E. Marsh, *Our Daily Bread* (Grand Rapids: RBC Ministries, 1977), August 7 entry.

2. *Pulpit Digest* (March/April 1978), 14.

Stephen F. Olford has served as a pastor in England and America and is also an international speaker and radio/TV personality. His Stephen Olford Center for Biblical Preaching in Memphis provides ongoing training in biblical preaching as well as resources for preachers. Dr. Olford is the author of numerous books.

Stephen Olford Center for Biblical Preaching

Our History

The Institute for Biblical Preaching was founded in 1980 to promote biblical preaching and practical training for pastors, evangelists, and lay leaders. After fifty years of pastoral and global ministry, Dr. Olford believes that the ultimate answer to the problems of every age is the anointed expository preaching of God's inerrant Word. Such preaching must be restored to the contemporary pulpit!

The Stephen Olford Center for Biblical Preaching was dedicated on June 4, 1988, in Memphis, Tennessee. It is the international headquarters for Encounter Ministries, Inc., and houses the Institute for Biblical Preaching.

Our Strategy

The purpose of the Institute for Biblical Preaching is to equip and encourage pastors and laymen in expository preaching and exemplary living, to the end that the church will be revived and the world will be reached with the saving Word of Christ. The program includes four basic activities:

- Institutes on expository preaching, pastoral leadership, essentials of evangelism, the fullness of the Holy Spirit, the reality of revival, and other related subjects.
- Workshops for pastors and laymen to preach "live" in order to have their sermons, skills, and styles critiqued constructively.
- 1-Day Video Institutes on Anointed Biblical Preaching hosted around the country for pastors and laymen who invite us.
- Consultations on pastoral and practical matters.

For further information write Encounter Ministries, P.O. Box 757800, Memphis, TN 38175-7800; call (901) 757-7977; fax (901) 757-1372; e-mail Olford@memphisonline.com; or visit our World Wide Web site at www.olford.org.